HAL•LEONARD®

BASS PLAY-ALONG

AUDIO ACCESS INCLUDED

VOL. 6

CLASSIC ROCK

PLAYBACK+
Speed • Pitch • Balance • Loop

To access audio, visit:
www.halleonard.com/mylibrary

Enter Code
1374-2648-6943-1973

ISBN 978-0-634-09004-2

HAL•LEONARD®

For all works contained herein:
Unauthorized copying, arranging, adapting, recording, Internet posting, public performance, or other distribution of the music in this publication is an infringement of copyright. Infringers are liable under the law.

Visit Hal Leonard Online at
www.halleonard.com

Contact us:
Hal Leonard
7777 West Bluemound Road
Milwaukee, WI 53213
Email: info@halleonard.com

In Europe, contact:
Hal Leonard Europe Limited
42 Wigmore Street
Marylebone, London, W1U 2RN
Email: info@halleonardeurope.com

In Australia, contact:
Hal Leonard Australia Pty. Ltd.
4 Lentara Court
Cheltenham, Victoria, 3192 Australia
Email: info@halleonard.com.au

contents

Page	Title
4	Free Ride
16	Funk #49
8	Gimme Three Steps
21	Green-Eyed Lady
26	Radar Love
42	Werewolves of London
35	White Room
48	Won't Get Fooled Again
63	BASS NOTATION LEGEND

Free Ride

Words and Music by Dan Hartman

© 1972, 1974 (Renewed 2000, 2002) EMI BLACKWOOD MUSIC INC.
All Rights Reserved International Copyright Secured Used by Permission

Chorus
F♯m G A F♯m G
come on and take a free ride. Come on and stand here

To Coda
D F♯m G D
by my side. Come on and take a free ride.

1., 2., 3.
4.
D.S. al Coda
Guitar Solo
A G D G D A D G D A
2. All

Coda
A G D G D A D A G D

1., 2., 3.
Guitar Solo
G D A D D C A D/A A5
Yeah, yeah, yeah, yeah.
4.
D/A A F♯m G A
(Ooh.
F♯m G D F♯m G D
Ooh.
Ooh.
Free ride.)
Interlude
N.C.
Play 4 times
Outro
w/ Voc. ad lib.
A G D G D A D
Come on and take a free ride.

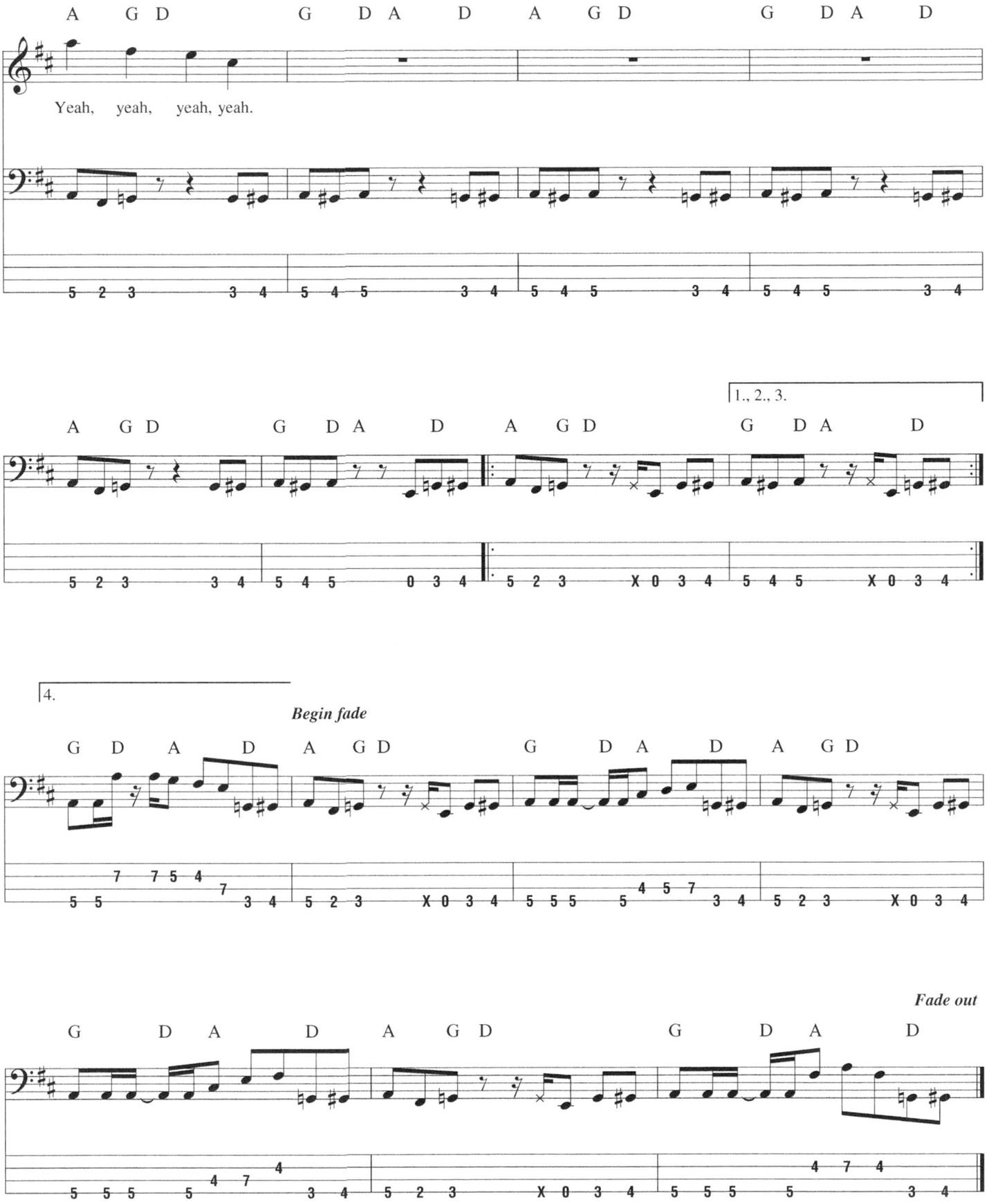

Additional Lyrics

2. All over the country I've seen it the same,
Nobody's winning at this kind of game.
We've gotta do better, it's time to begin.
You know all the answers must come from within.

Gimme Three Steps

Words and Music by Allen Collins and Ronnie Van Zant

Copyright © 1973, 1976 SONGS OF UNIVERSAL, INC.
Copyrights Renewed
All Rights Reserved Used by Permission

E7
D
A
D
Verse
D
1. I was cut - tin' the rug down at a
A7
place called The Jug with a girl named Lin - da Lu when
D
E7
A7
in walked a man with a gun in his hand and he was look-ing for you know who.

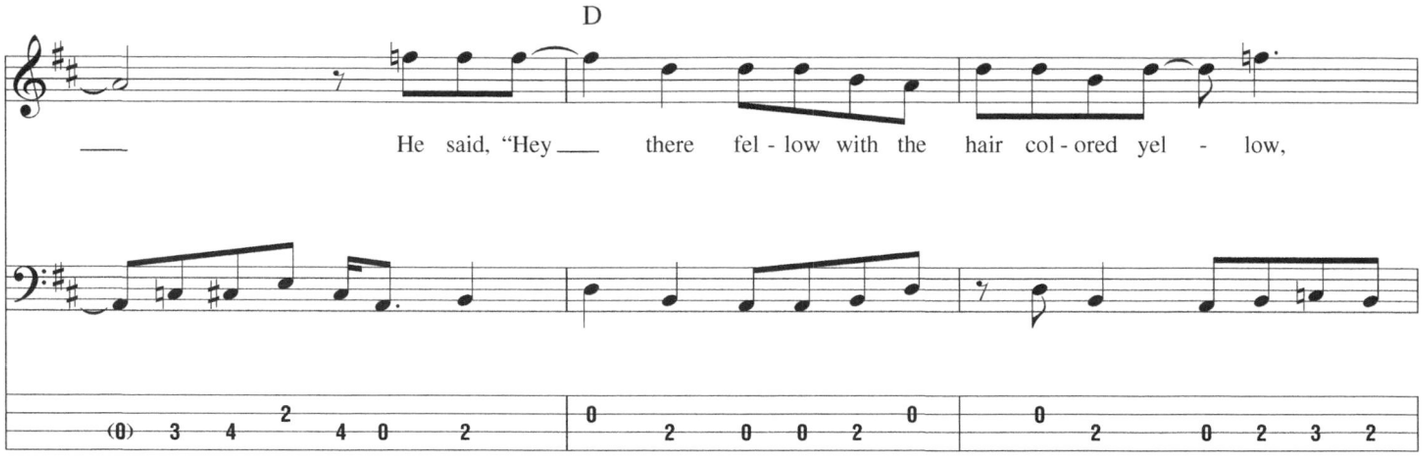
D
He said, "Hey there fel - low with the hair col - ored yel - low,

G
E7
D
what you try - in' to prove?
'Cause that's my wom - an there and I'm a

A7
D
man who cares and this might be all for you."

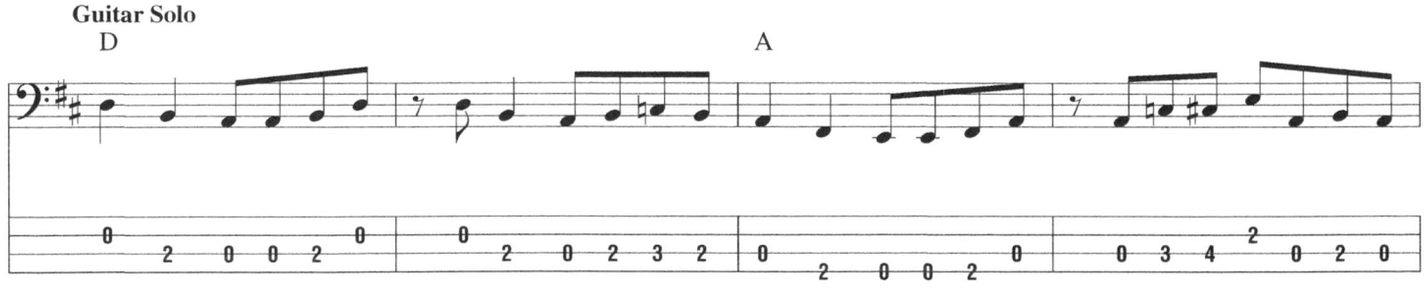
Guitar Solo
D
A

D
A
D

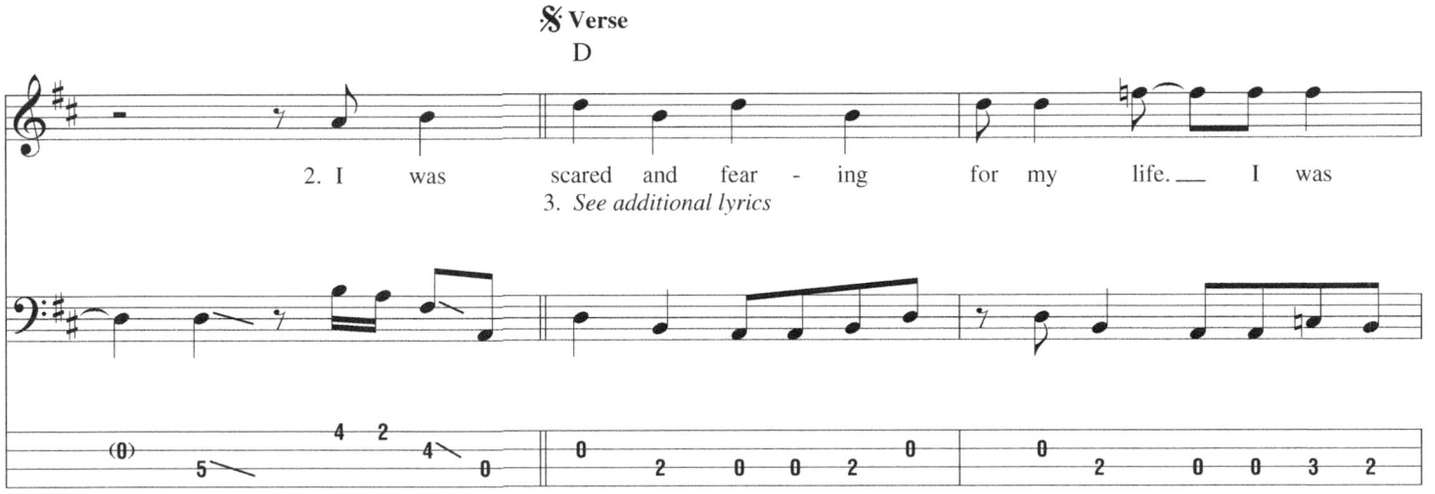
Verse
D
2. I was scared and fear - ing for my life. I was
3. See additional lyrics

A7
D
sha - kin' like a leaf on a tree. 'Cause he was lean, mean,

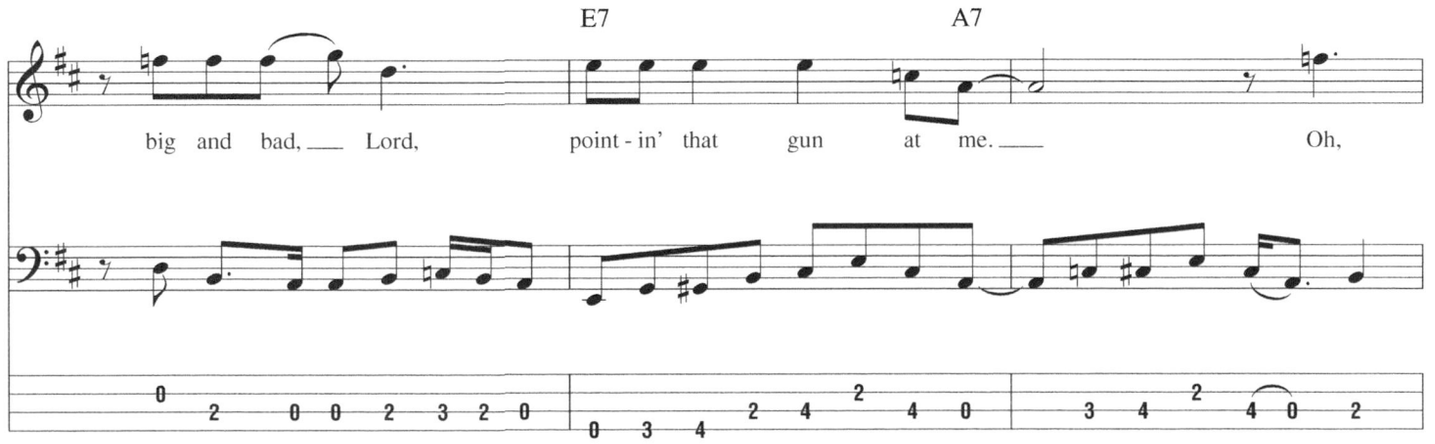
E7
A7
big and bad, Lord, point - in' that gun at me. Oh,

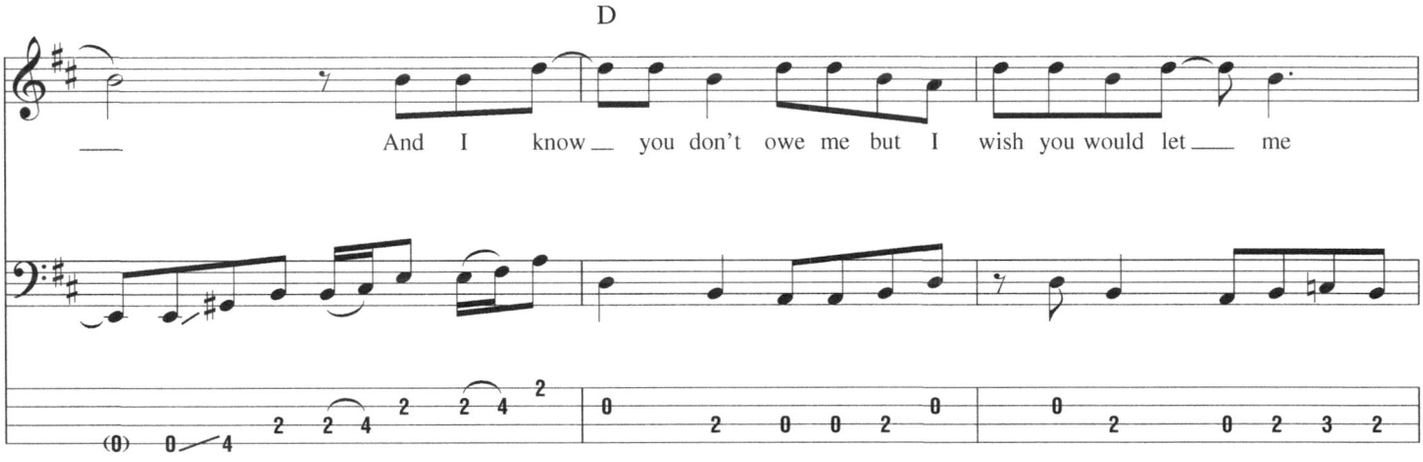

2nd time, substitute Fill 1

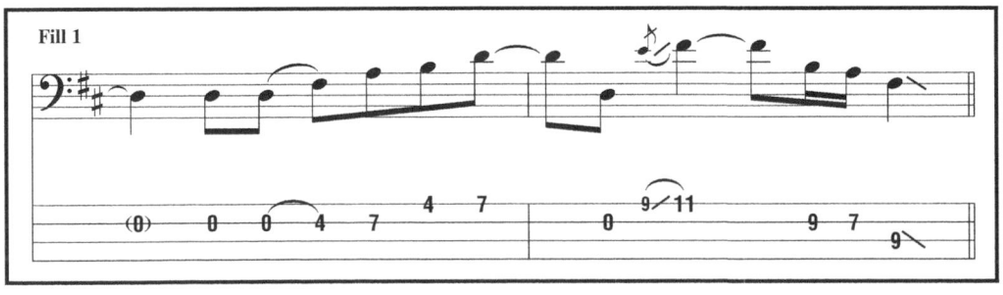

Chorus
D
A7
gim - me three steps, gim - me three steps, mis - ter. Gim - me three steps to - ward the door.
D
Gim - me three steps, gim - me three steps, mis - ter, and you'll
A7
D
To Coda
nev - er see me no more.
Guitar Solo
D
A

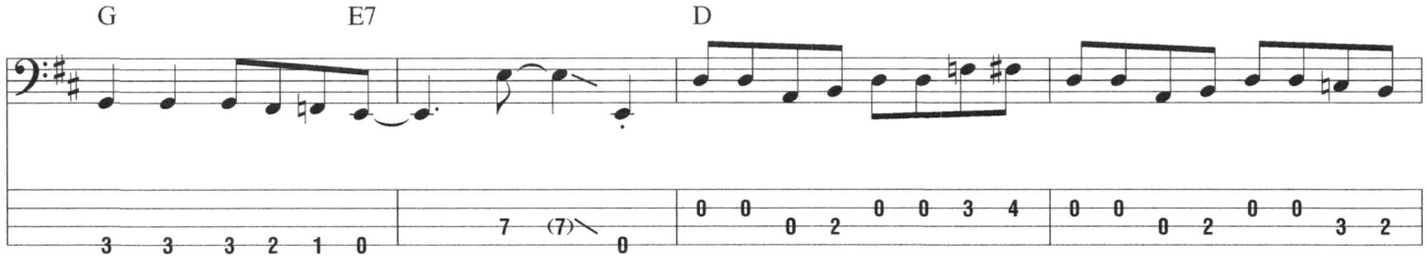

D.S. al Coda

Coda

Outro-Guitar Solo

Additional Lyrics

3. Well, the crowd cleared away and I began to pray
And the water fell on the floor.
And I'm tellin' you, son, well, it ain't no fun
Starin' straight down a forty-four.
Well, he turned and screamed at Linda Lu
And that's the break I was lookin' for.
And you could hear me screamin' a mile away
As I was headin' out t'wards the door.

Funk #49

Words and Music by Joe Walsh, Dale Peters and James Fox

Copyright © 1970 SONGS OF UNIVERSAL, INC. and HOME MADE MUSIC
Copyright Renewed
All Rights Controlled and Administered by SONGS OF UNIVERSAL, INC.
All Rights Reserved Used by Permission

Interlude
N.C.
A5
N.C.
A5
N.C.
B5
N.C.
B5
N.C.
E7♯9
A7
D/A
A7
D/A G/B D/A
A7
2. A
𝄋 Verse
A7
D/A
A7
D/A G/B D/A
A7
jump-in' up, fall - in' down, don't mis - un - der - stand me.
3. See additional lyrics

Interlude

To Coda

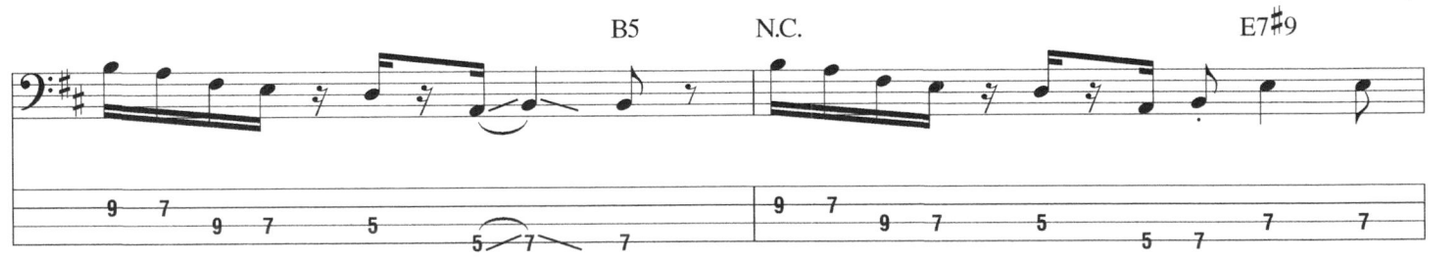

Percussion Solo
Guitar Break
16
2
A7
D/A A7
D/A
A7
D.S. al Coda
D/A
A7
D/A
A7
Coda
Outro
A7
D/A A7
D/A G/B D/A
A7
D/A A7
D/A G/B D/A
A7
D/A A7
D/A G/B D/A
A7
D/A A7
D/A G/B D/A
A7

Begin fade

Fade out

Additional Lyrics

3. Out all night, sleep all day,
I know what you're doin'.
If you're gonna act this way,
I think there's trouble brewin'.

Green-Eyed Lady

Words and Music by Jerry Corbetta, J.C. Phillips and David Riordan

Intro
Moderately fast ♩ = 152

N.C. Em7 Em6 N.C.

mf

*Key signature denotes E Dorian.

Em7 Em N.C. Em D G A

Em Em7

N.C.(Em7) (A7/E)

(Am7/E) (Em7)

© 1970 (Renewed) CLARIDGE MUSIC COMPANY, A Division of MPL Music Publishing, Inc.
All Rights Reserved

Verse
Em7
A7/E
1. Green-eyed la - dy, love-ly la - dy. Stroll - ing
2. See additional lyrics
Am7/E
Em7
slow - ly to - wards the sun.
A7/E
Green-eyed la - dy, o - cean la - dy. Sooth - ing
Am7/E
Em7
ev - 'ry rag - ing wave that comes.

A7/E
Green-eyed la-dy, pas-sions la-dy. Dressed in

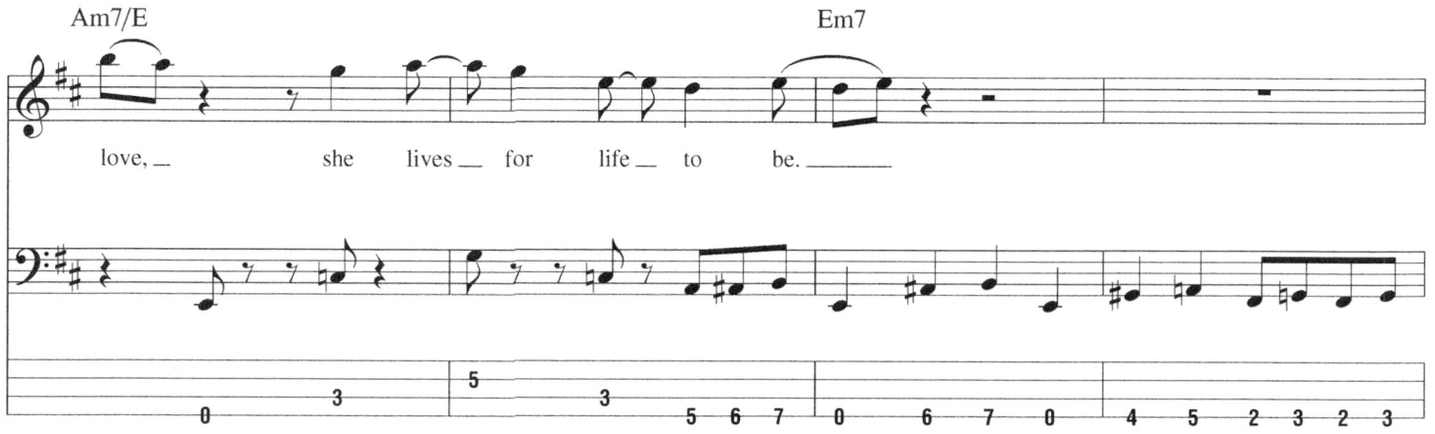
Am7/E
Em7
love, she lives for life to be.

A7/E
Green-eyed la-dy feels life, I nev-er see set-ting

To Coda ⊕

Am7/E
Em7
suns and lone-ly lov-ers free.

Organ Solo
Em7
F♯m7 Gmaj7
F♯m7
Em7
F♯m7
Gmaj7
1., 2., 3.
4.
F♯m7
F♯m7
Em7
F♯m7 Gmaj7
F♯m7
Em7
Guitar Solo
F♯m7
Gmaj7
F♯m7
N.C.(Em7)
(B/E)
(B7/E)

Additional Lyrics

2. Green-eyed lady, wind-swept Lady.
Rules the night, the waves, the sand.
Green-eyed lady, ocean lady.
Child of nature, friend of man.
Green-eyed lady, passions lady.
Dressed in love, she lives for life to be.
Green-eyed lady feels life,
I never see setting suns and lovely lovers free.

Radar Love

Words and Music by George Kooymans and Barry Hay

Copyright © 1973 Snamyook
Copyright Renewed
All Rights Administered by Sony/ATV Music Publishing, 8 Music Square West, Nashville, TN 37203
International Copyright Secured All Rights Reserved

Verse
N.C.(F♯m)
- in' all night, my hand's wet on the wheel.
There's a voice
2. See additional lyrics
in my head that drives my heel.
It's my ba -
- by call - in', says, "I need you here."
And it's a
half past four and I'm shift - in' gear.

Pre-Chorus
E5
B5
F♯5
E5
When she is lone - ly and the long - ing gets too much, she sends a ca -
See additional lyrics
B5
A5/B
B5/C♯
C♯5
B5/C♯
- ble com - ing in from a - bove. Don't need a phone at all.
Chorus
D
A5
E5
F♯5
We've got a thing, and that's a called ra - dar love.
To Coda
D
A5
E5
N.C.
We've got a wave in the air.
We've got a light in the sky.
Ra - dar

Interlude
N.C.(F♯m7)
love.

1., 2.
3.
D.S. al Coda
2. The

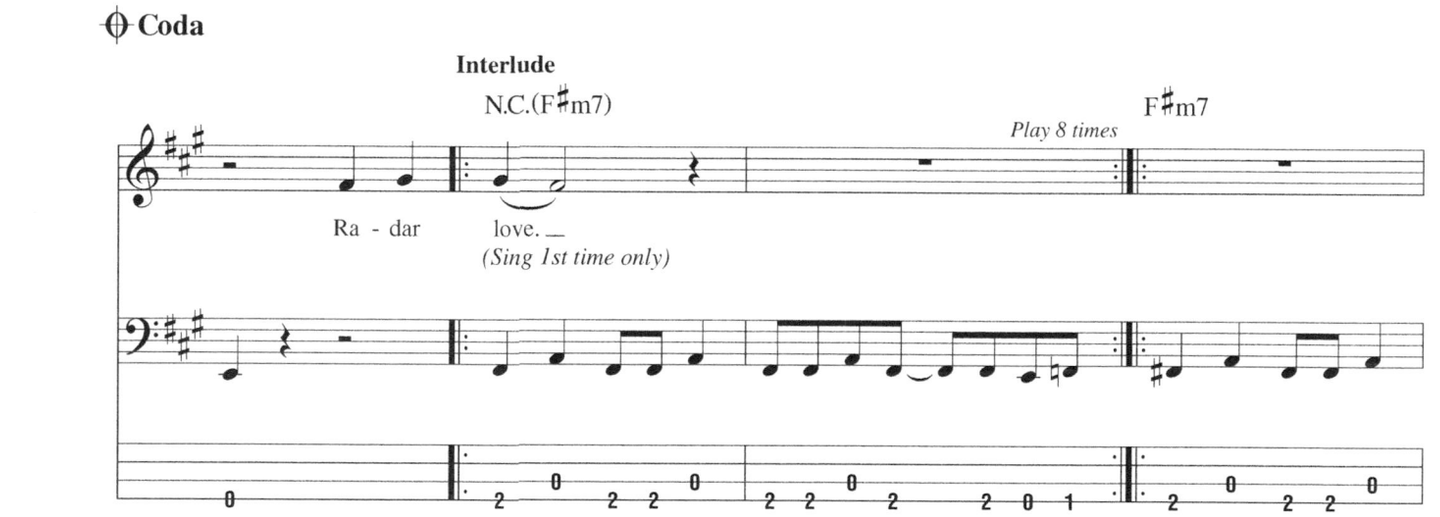
Coda
Interlude
N.C.(F♯m7)
F♯m7
Play 8 times
Ra - dar
love.
(Sing 1st time only)

Play 24 times
C♯5

Breakdown
N.C.
(Drums)
8
Play 4 times
E5
Interlude
N.C.(F♯m7)
Play 3 times

Verse
N.C.(F♯m7)
3. No more speed, I'm al - most there.
Got - ta keep cool now, got - ta take care.
Last car to pass, here I go!
And the
line of cars drove down real slow, whoa.
And the

ra - di - o played that for - got - ten song.
Bren - da Lee, it's com - in' on strong.
And the
news man sang his same song.
Oh,
one more ra - dar lov - er gone.

Pre-Chorus
E5
B5
F♯5
E5
When I get lone - ly and I'm sure I've had e - nough, she sends a com -
B5
A5/B
B5/C♯
C♯5
B5/C♯
- fort com - ing in from a - bove. We don't need no let-ter at all.
Chorus
D
A5
E5
F♯5
We've got a thing that's called ra - dar love.
D
A5
E5
F♯5
We've got a light in the sky.

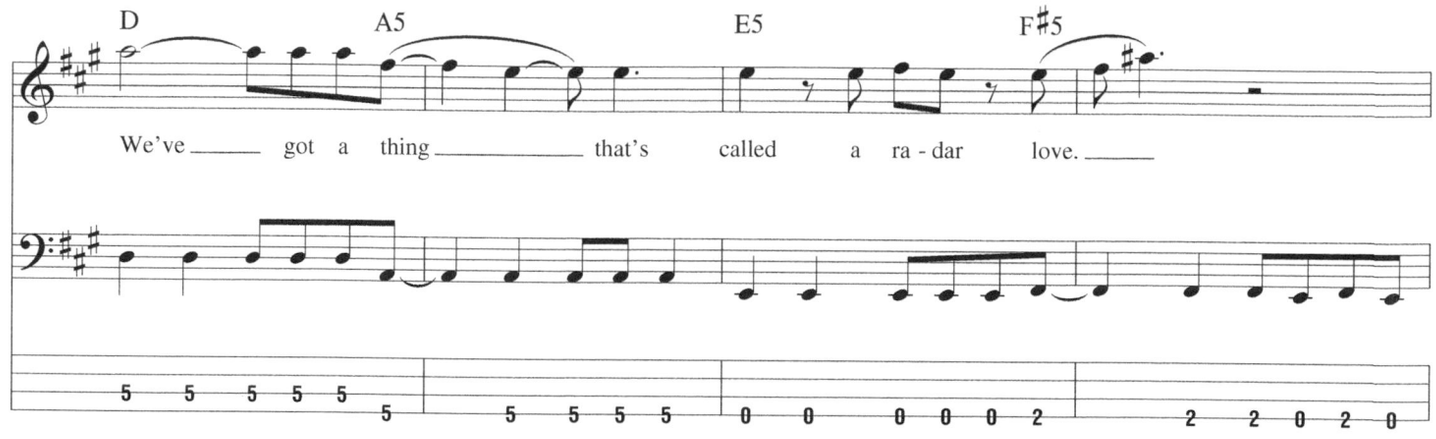

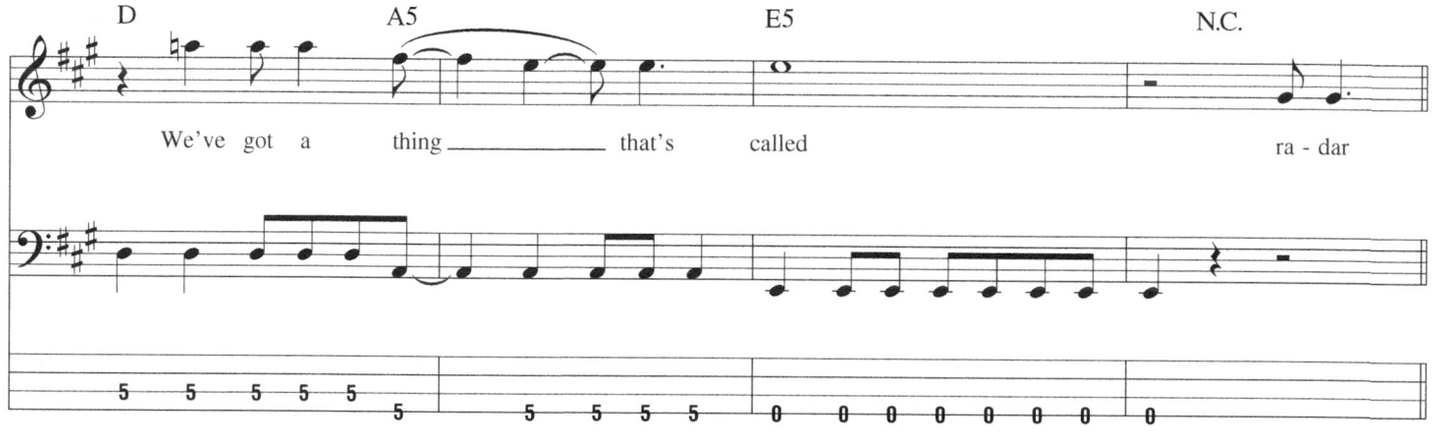

Additional Lyrics

2. The radio's playin' some forgotten song.
Brenda Lee comin' on strong.
The road has got me hypnotized,
And I'm spinnin' into a new sunrise.

Pre-Chorus When I get lonely and I'm sure I've had enough,
She sends a comfort coming in from above.
We don't need no letter at all.

White Room

Words and Music by Jack Bruce and Pete Brown

Copyright © 1968 by Dratleaf Ltd.
Copyright Renewed
All Rights Administered by Unichappell Music Inc.
International Copyright Secured All Rights Reserved

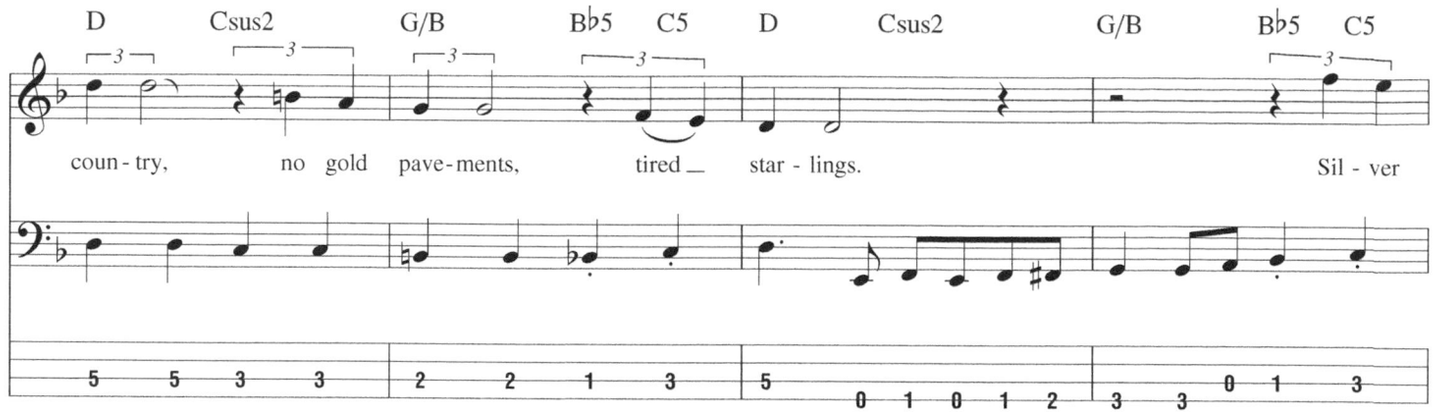
D Csus2 G/B B♭5 C5 D Csus2 G/B B♭5 C5
coun - try, no gold pave - ments, tired star - lings. Sil - ver

D Csus2 G/B B♭5 C5 D Csus2 G/B B♭5 C5
hors - es ran down moon-beams in your dark eyes. Dawn-light

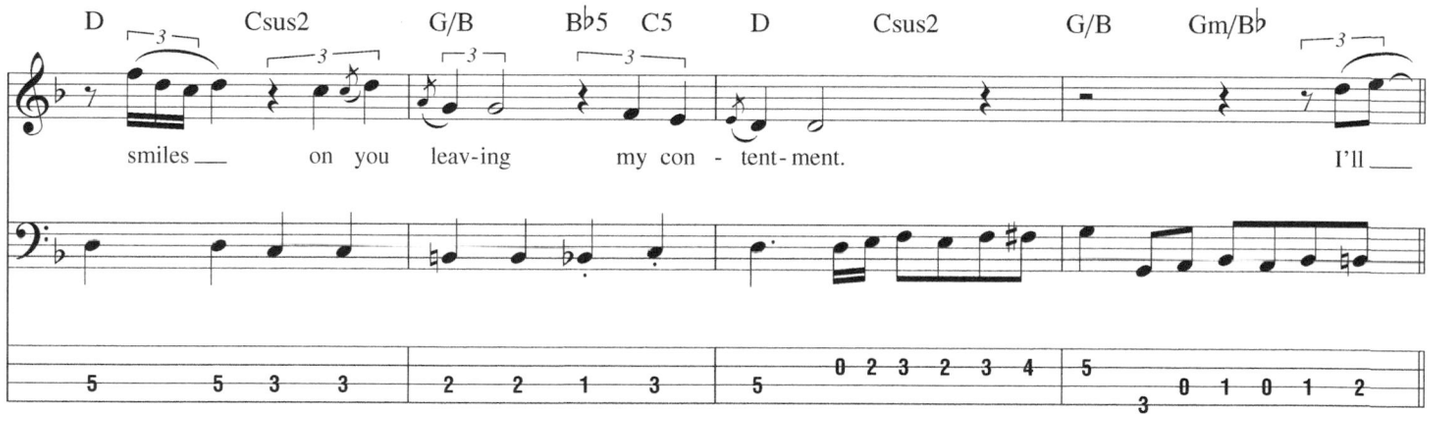
D Csus2 G/B B♭5 C5 D Csus2 G/B Gm/B♭
smiles on you leav-ing my con - tent-ment. I'll

Bridge

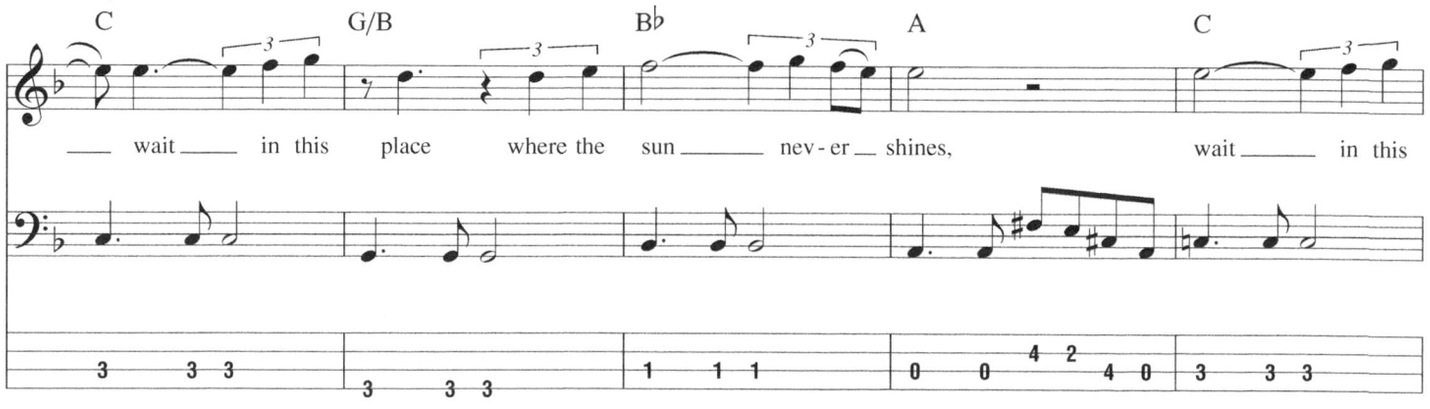
C G/B B♭ A C
wait in this place where the sun nev - er shines, wait in this

G/B
B♭
C
D
N.C.
place where the shad - ows run from them - selves.
2. You said

Verse

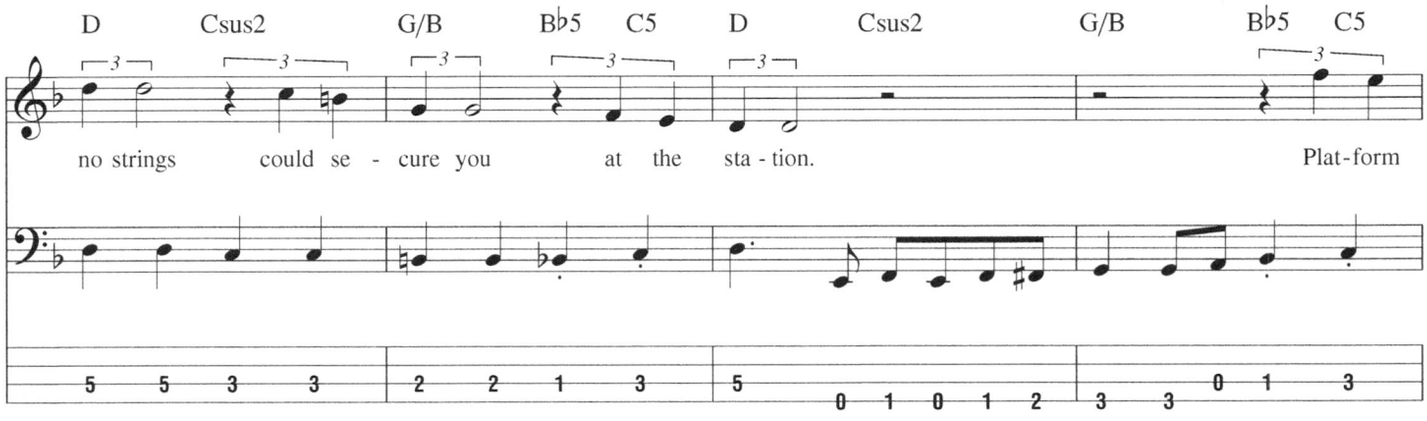
D Csus2 G/B B♭5 C5 D Csus2 G/B B♭5 C5
no strings could se - cure you at the sta - tion.
Plat-form

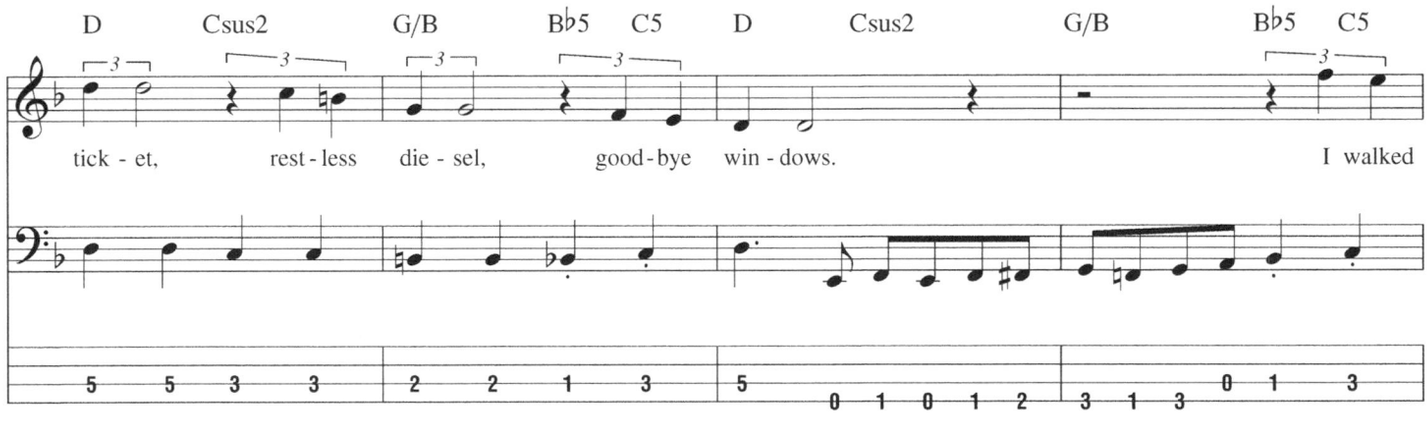
D Csus2 G/B B♭5 C5 D Csus2 G/B B♭5 C5
tick - et, rest - less die - sel, good - bye win - dows.
I walked

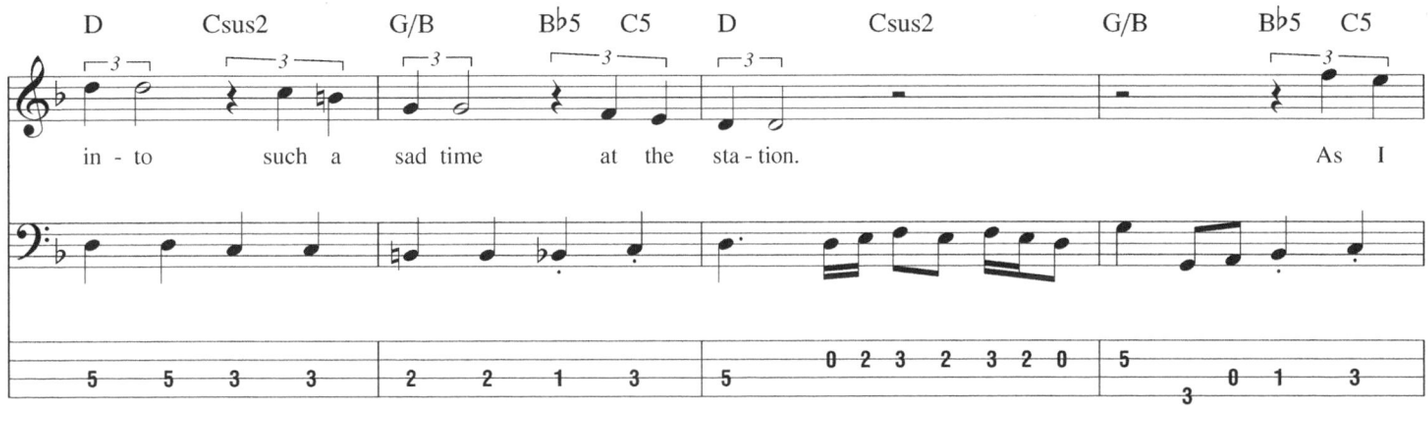
D Csus2 G/B B♭5 C5 D Csus2 G/B B♭5 C5
in - to such a sad time at the sta - tion.
As I

D Csus2 G/B B♭5 C5 D Csus2 G/B Gm/B♭
walked out, felt my own need just be - gin-ning. I'll

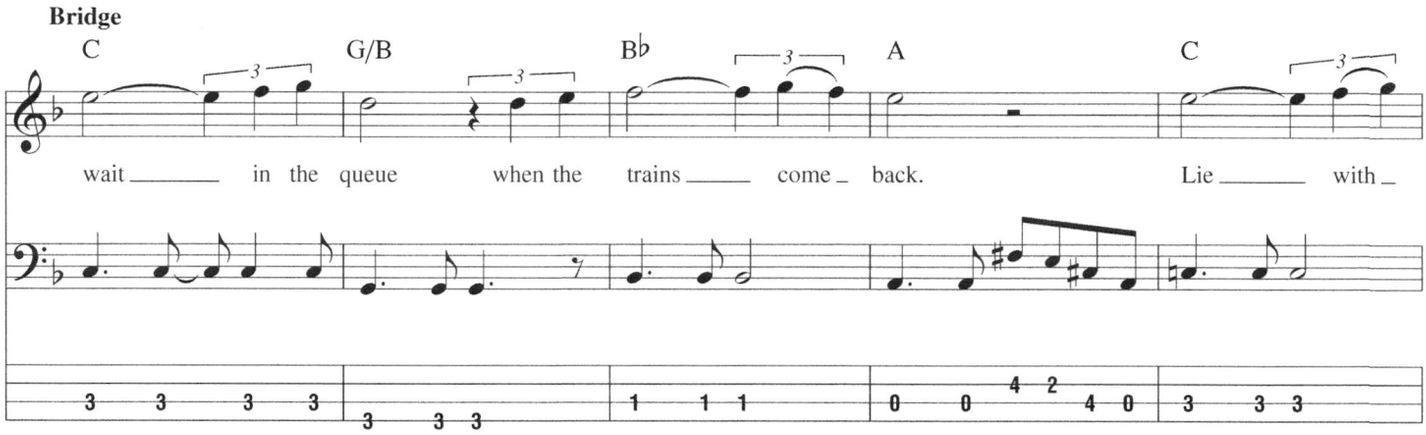
Bridge
C G/B B♭ A C
wait in the queue when the trains come back. Lie with

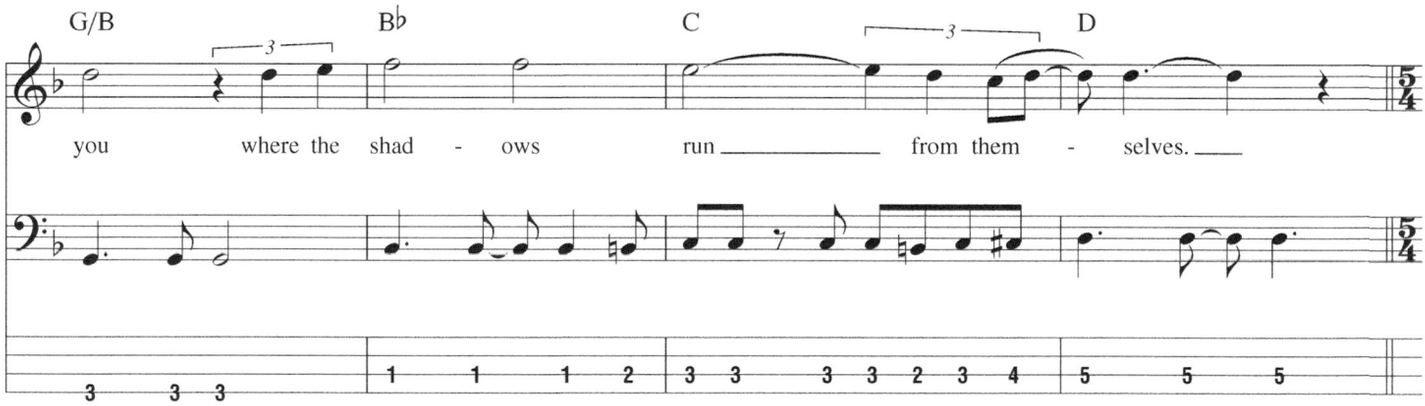
G/B B♭ C D
you where the shad - ows run from them - selves.

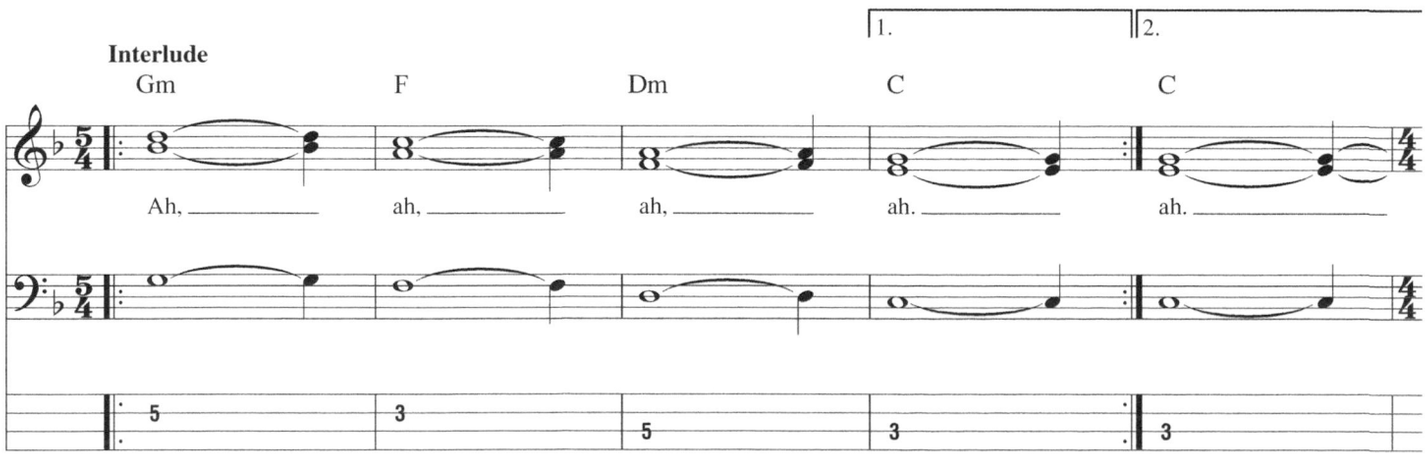
Interlude
Gm F Dm C C
1. 2.
Ah, ah, ah, ah. ah.

Verse
Am7 D Csus2 G/B B♭5 C5 D Csus2
3. At the par - ty she was kind - ness in the hard crowd.
G/B B♭5 C5 D Csus2 G/B B♭5 C5 D Csus2
I - so - la - tion for the old queen now for - got - ten.
G/B B♭5 C5 D Csus2 G/B B♭5 C5 D Csus2
Yel - low ti - gers crouched in jun - gles in her dark eyes.
G/B B♭5 C5 D Csus2 G/B B♭5 C5 D Csus2
She's just dress - ing good - bye win - dows, tired star - ling.

Bridge
G/B
Gm/B♭
C
G/B
B♭
I'll sleep in this place with the lone - ly
A
C
G/B
B♭
crowd. Lie in the dark, where the shad - ows
C
D
run from them - selves.
Interlude
Gm
F
Ah, ah,
Dm
1.
C
2.
C
Am7
ah, ah. ah.

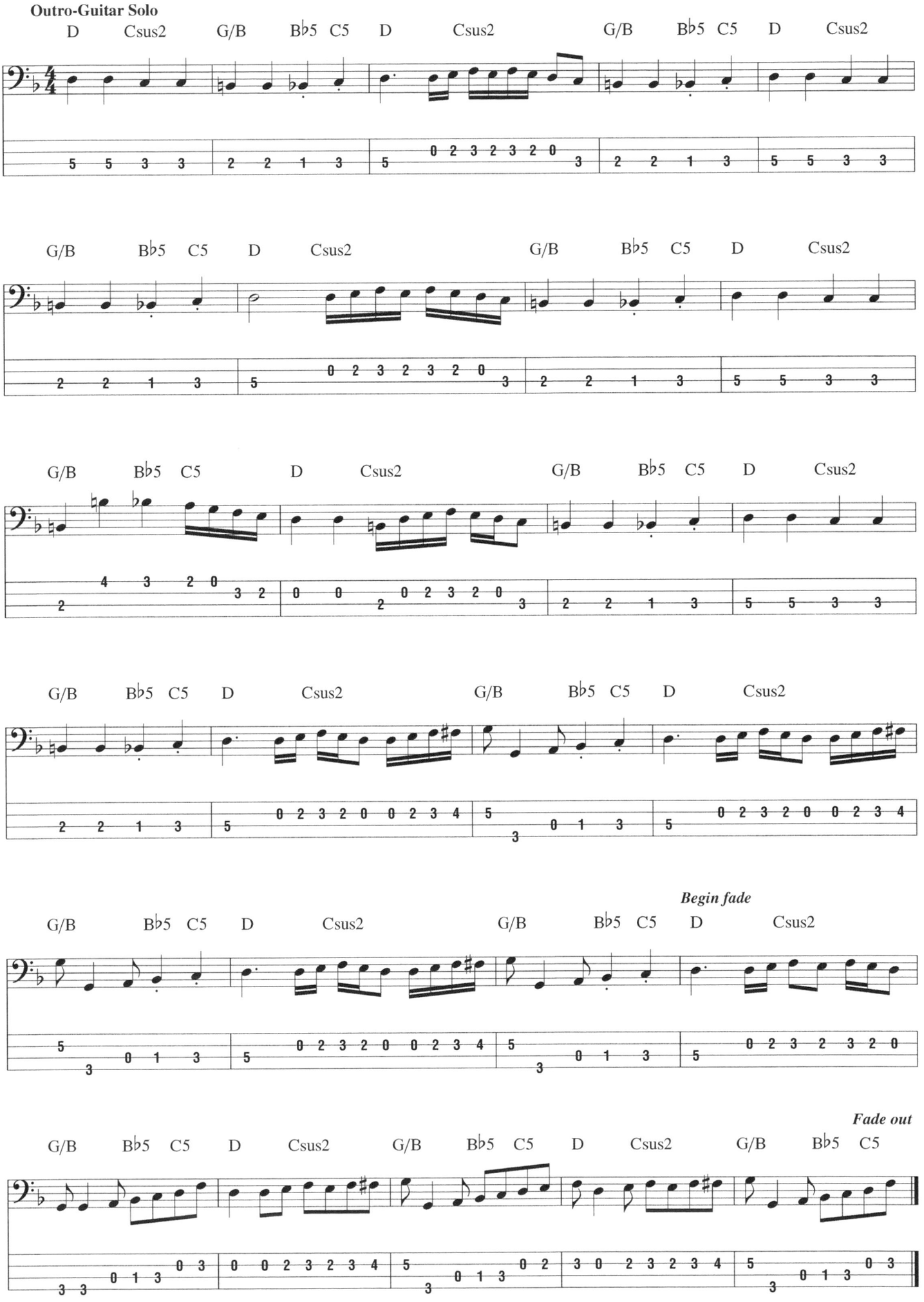
Outro-Guitar Solo
D Csus2 G/B B♭5 C5 D Csus2 G/B B♭5 C5 D Csus2
G/B B♭5 C5 D Csus2 G/B B♭5 C5 D Csus2
G/B B♭5 C5 D Csus2 G/B B♭5 C5 D Csus2
G/B B♭5 C5 D Csus2 G/B B♭5 C5 D Csus2
Begin fade
G/B B♭5 C5 D Csus2 G/B B♭5 C5 D Csus2
Fade out
G/B B♭5 C5 D Csus2 G/B B♭5 C5 D Csus2 G/B B♭5 C5

Werewolves of London

Words and Music by Warren Zevon, Robert Wachtel and LeRoy Marinel

© 1978, 1979 EMI VIRGIN MUSIC LTD. and TINY TUNES MUSIC
All Rights for EMI VIRGIN MUSIC LTD. Controlled and Administered by EMI VIRGIN SONGS, INC.
All Rights for TINY TUNES MUSIC Administered by MUSIC & MEDIA INTERNATIONAL
All Rights Reserved International Copyright Secured Used by Permission

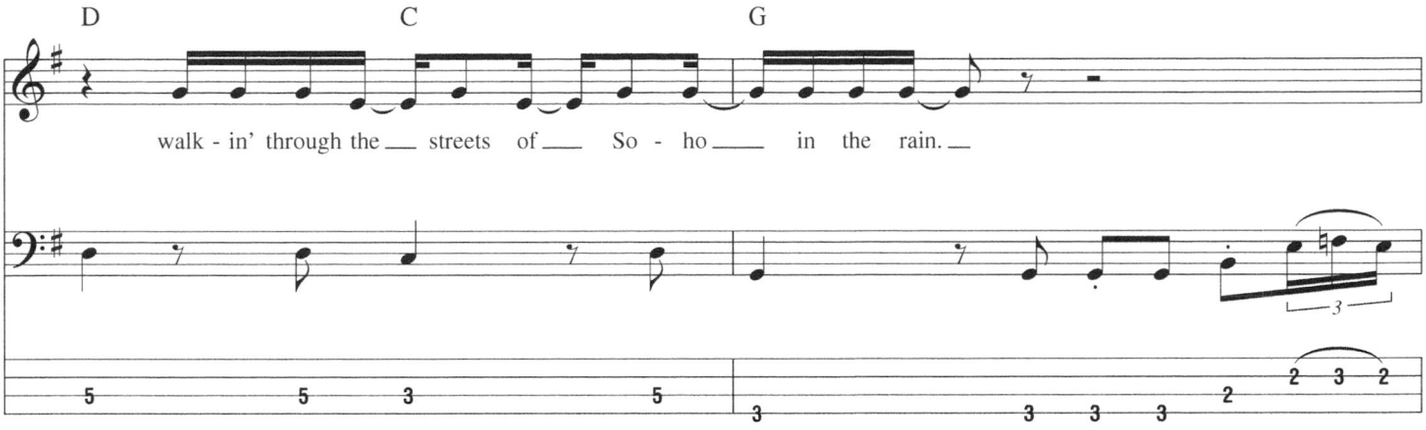
D C G
walk - in' through the streets of So - ho in the rain.

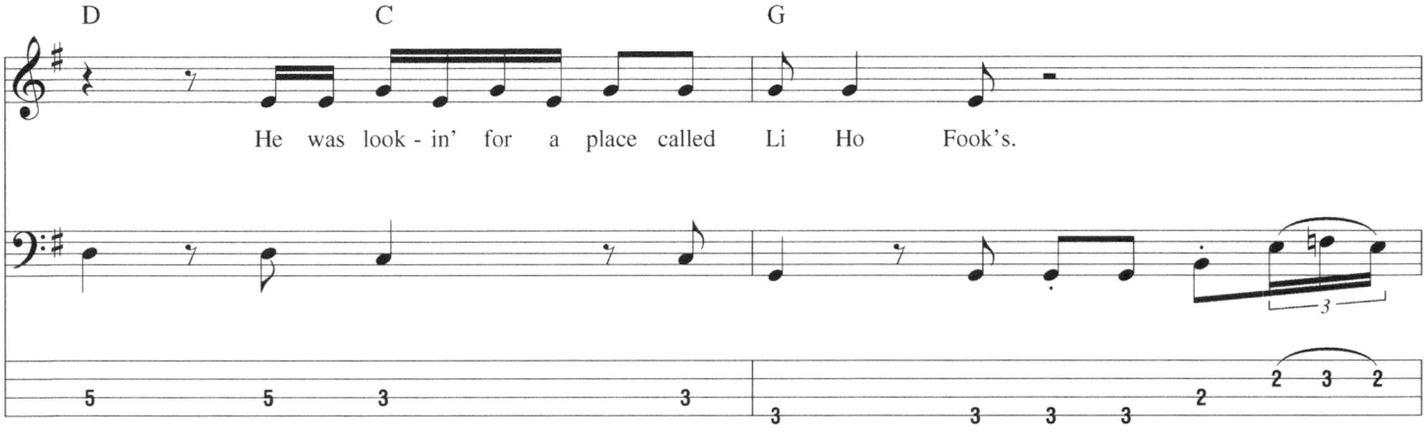
D C G
He was look - in' for a place called Li Ho Fook's.

D C G
Wan - na get a big dish of beef chow mein.

Chorus

D C G D C
Ow ooh, were - wolves of Lon - don, ow ooh.

To Coda
G D C G
Ow ooh, were - wolves of Lon - don,
D C G G
1. 2.
ow ooh.
Huh!
Guitar Solo
D C G D C G
D C G D C G
D.S. al Coda
3. He's been

Coda
D C G
ow ooh.
Verse
D C G
4. I saw Lon Cha - ney walk - in' with the Queen
D C G
do - in' the were - wolves of Lon - don.
D C G
I saw Lon Cha - ney jun - ior walk - in' with the Queen, uh,

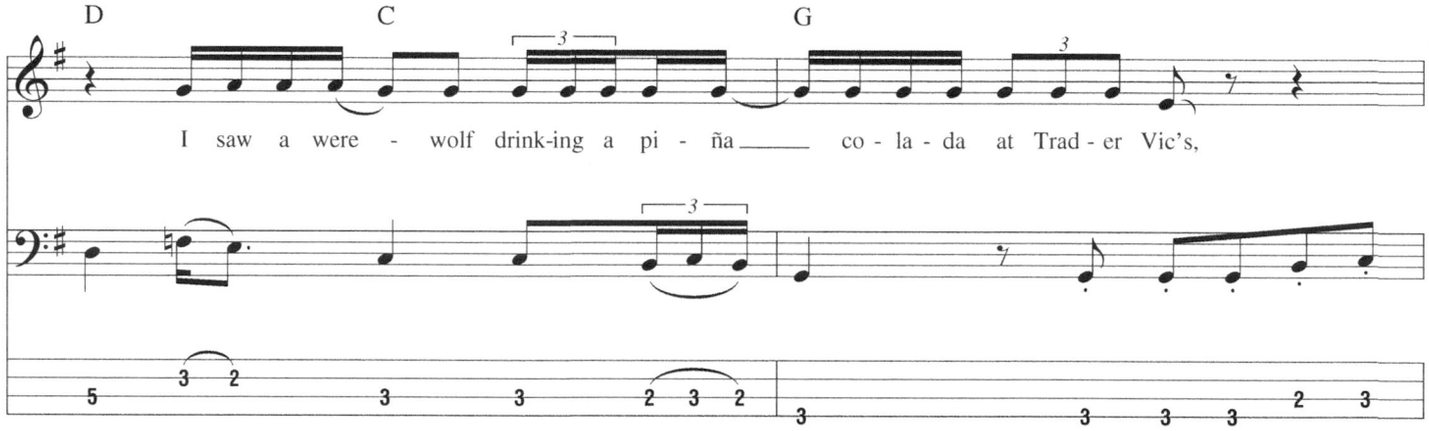

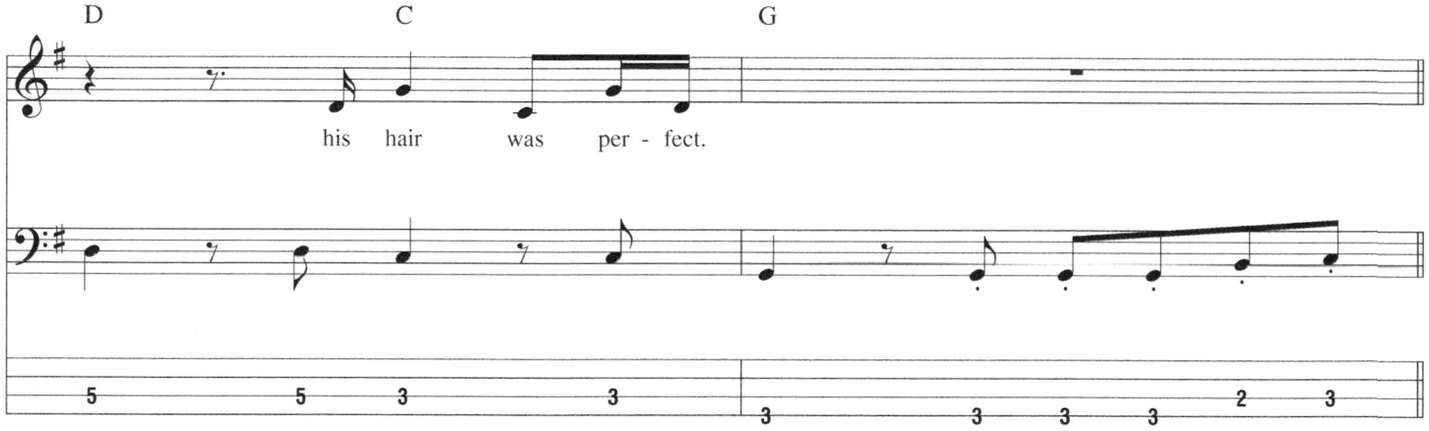

Outro-Chorus

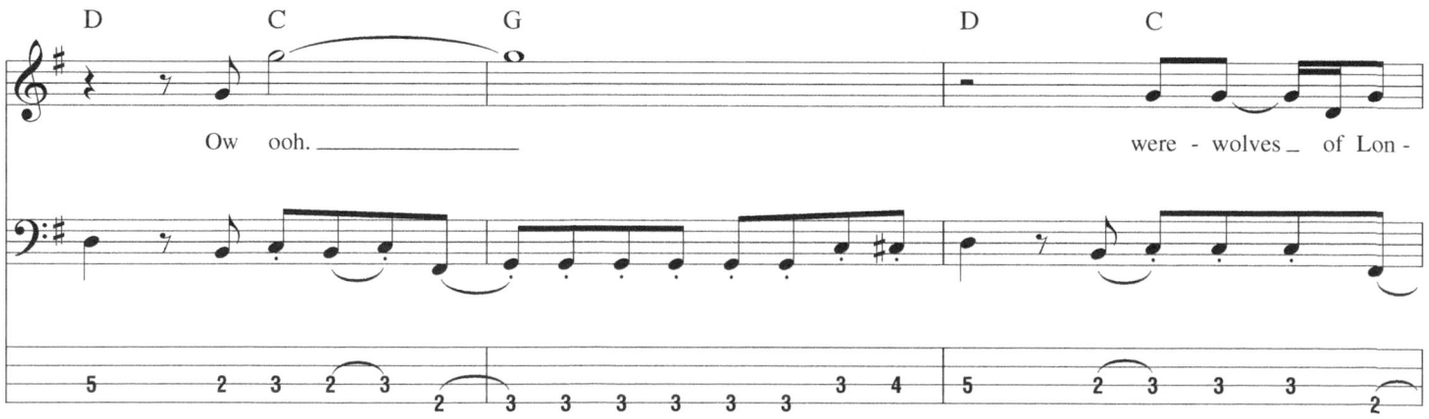

Additional Lyrics

2. You hear him howlin' around your kitchen door.
   You better not let him in.
   Little old lady got mutilated late last night.
   Werewolves of London again.

3. He's been a heavy handed gent who ran amuck in Kent.
   Lately he's been overheard in Mayfair.
   You better stay away from him, he'll rip your lungs out, Jim.
   Huh! I'd like to meet his tailor.

Won't Get Fooled Again

Words and Music by Pete Townshend

Copyright © 1971 Towser Tunes Inc., ABKCO Music Inc. and Fabulous Music Ltd.
Copyright Renewed
All Rights for Towser Tunes Inc. throughout the world Administered by BMG Music Publishing International
All Rights for BMG Music Publishing International in the U.S. Administered by Careers-BMG Music Publishing
International Copyright Secured All Rights Reserved

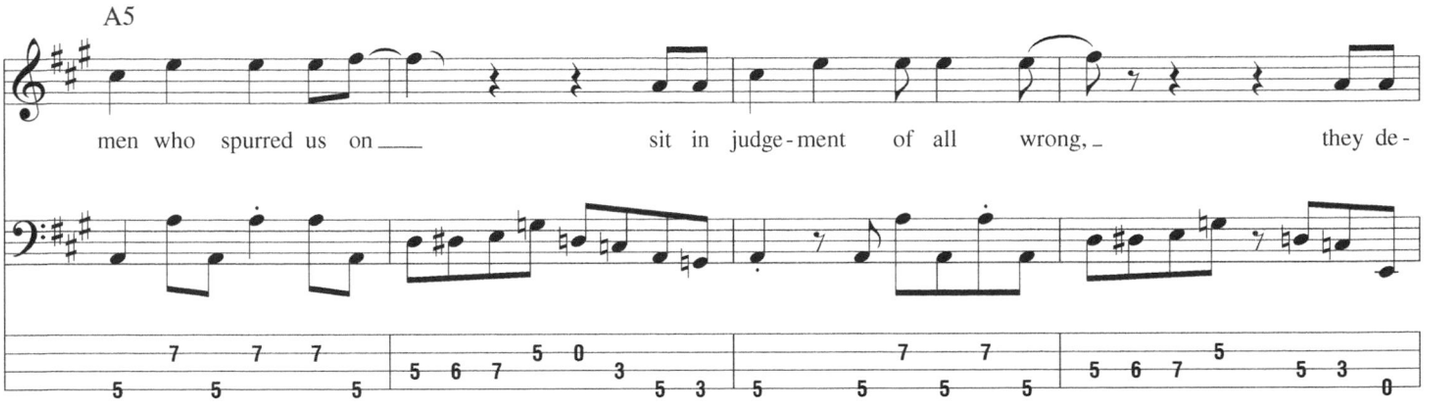
A5
men who spurred us on
sit in judge-ment of all wrong,
they de-

E
C/G G5/D
cide and the shot - gun sings the song.
I'll

Chorus

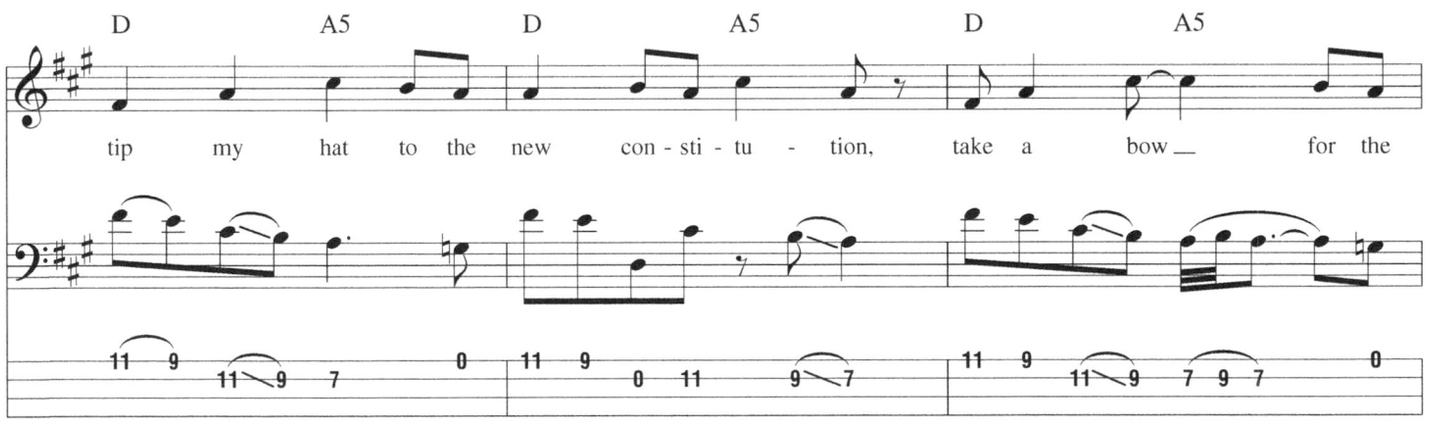
D A5 D A5 D A5
tip my hat to the new con - sti - tu - tion, take a bow
for the

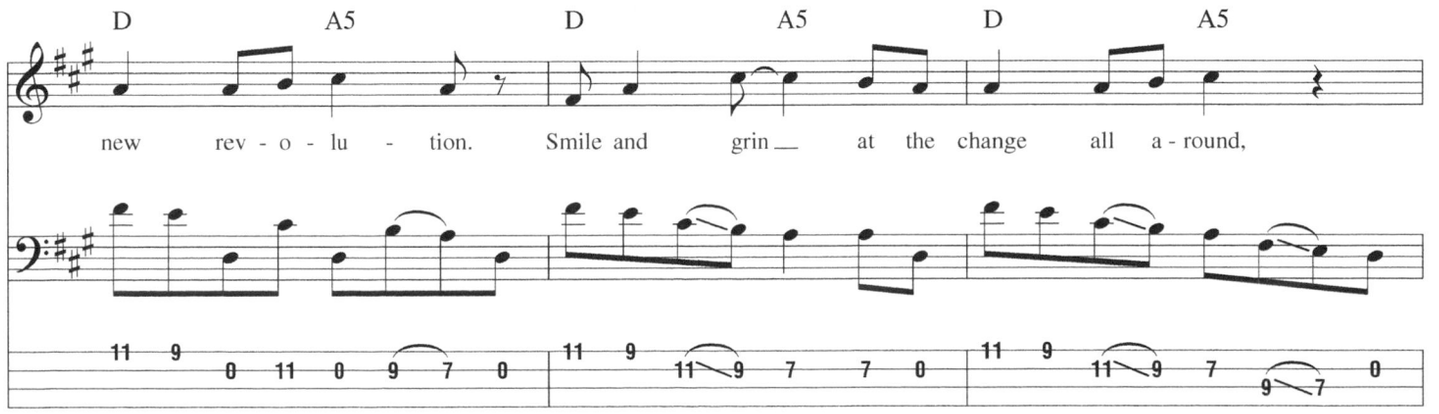
D A5 D A5 D A5
new rev - o - lu - tion. Smile and grin
at the change all a - round,

G
E
G
pick up my gui - tar and play,
just like yes - ter - day,

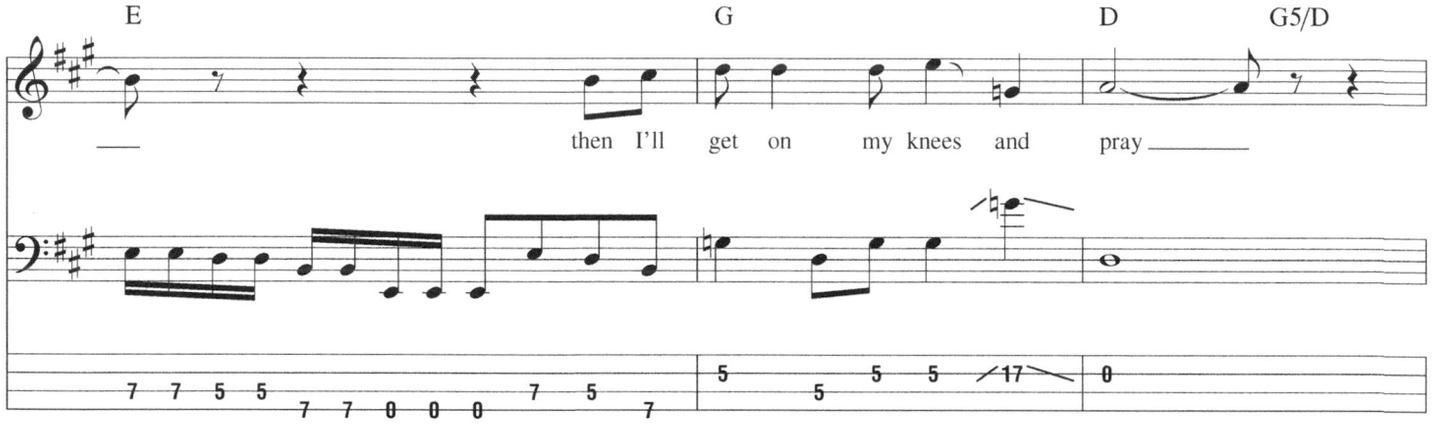
E
G
D
G5/D
then I'll get on my knees and pray

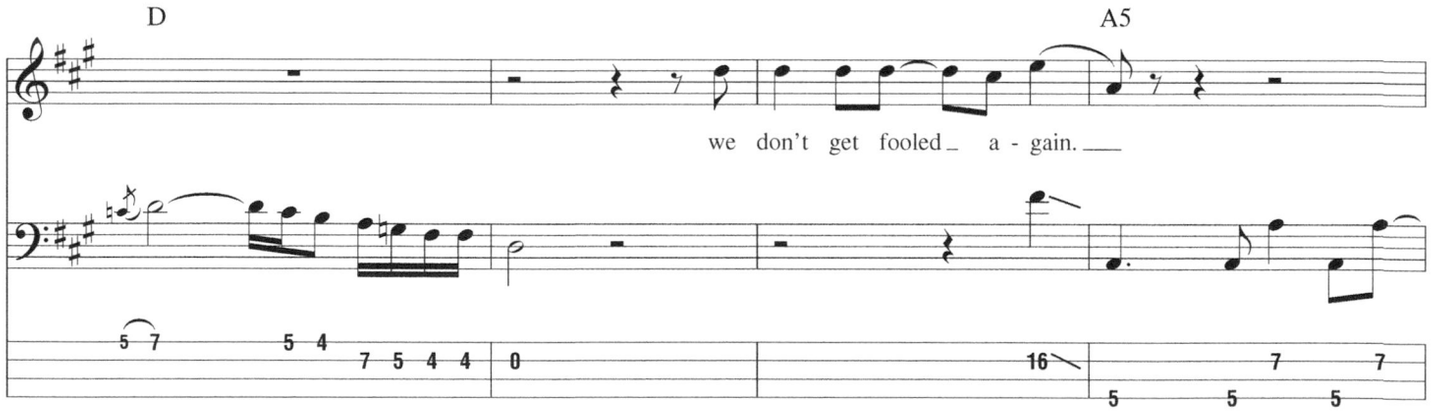
D
A5
we don't get fooled a - gain.

G5
D
A5
G5
D
A5

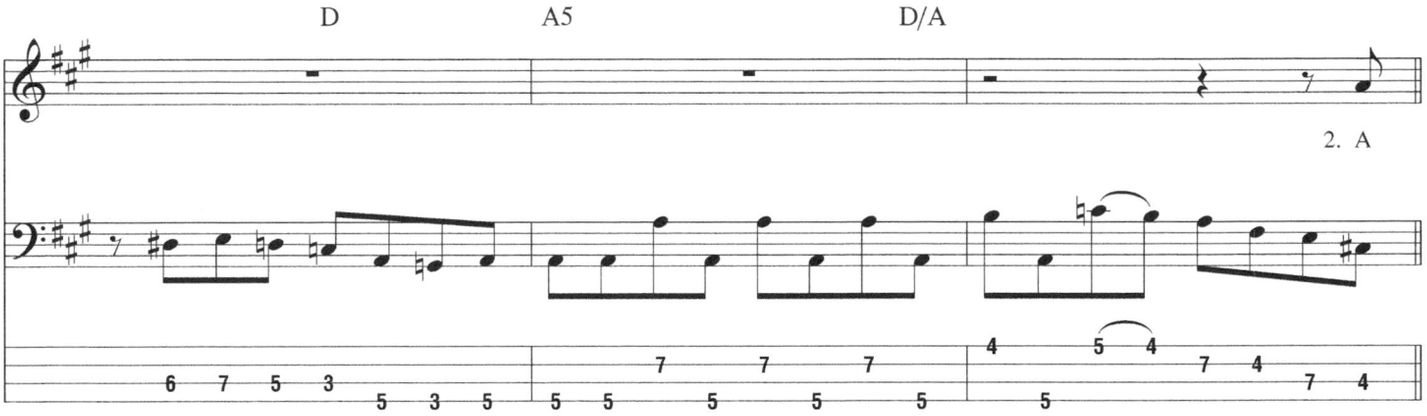
D
A5
D/A
2. A

Verse

A5
change, it had to come. We knew it all a - long. We were

E
C/G G5/D
lib - er - at - ed from the fold, that's all. And the

A5
world looks just the same, and his - to - ry ain't changed, 'cause the

E
C/G G5/D
ban - ners, they are flown in the last war. I'll

Chorus

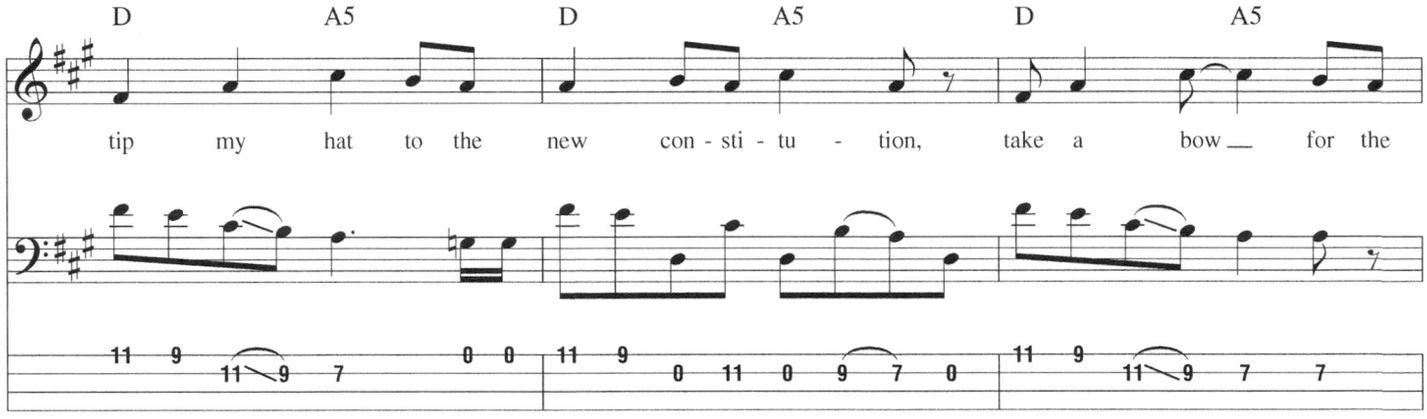
D A5 D A5 D A5
tip my hat to the new con - sti - tu - tion, take a bow for the

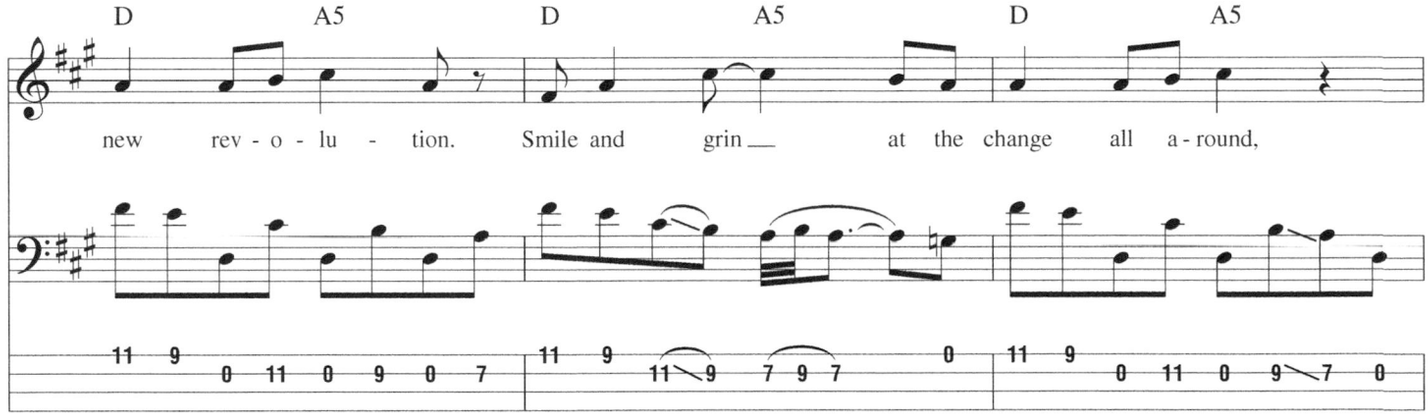
D A5 D A5 D A5
new rev - o - lu - tion. Smile and grin at the change all a - round,

G E G E
pick up my gui-tar and play, just like yes - ter - day, then I'll

G
D
G5/D
D
G5/D
get on my knees and pray
let ring
Dm7
A5
G5
D
we don't get fooled a - gain.
No no!
A5
G5
A5
G5
D
A5
G5
D
A5
G5
D
A5
G5
D5
A5
D/A

A5
D/A
A5

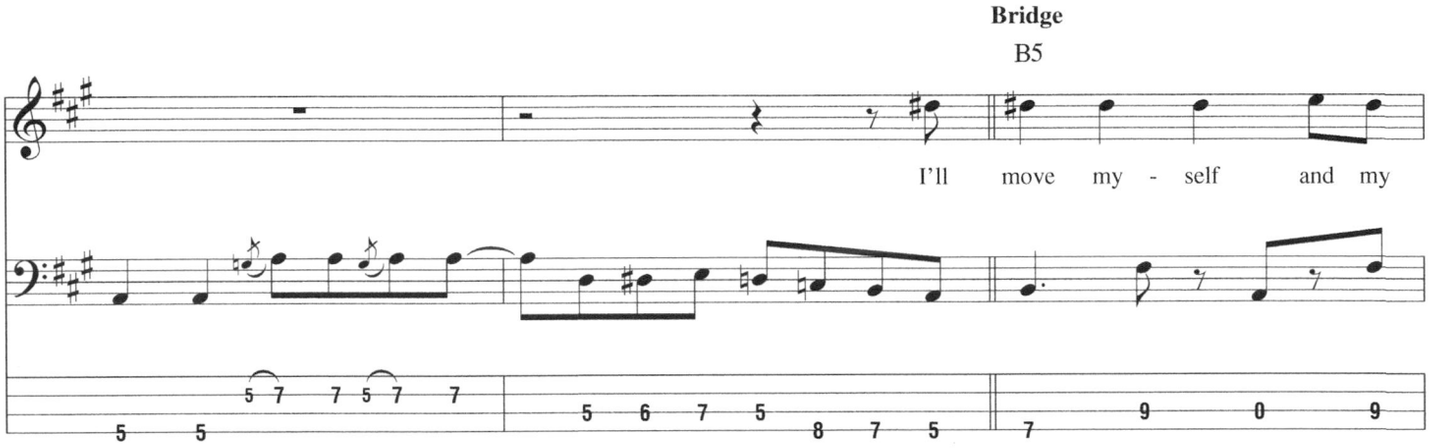
Bridge
B5
I'll move my - self and my

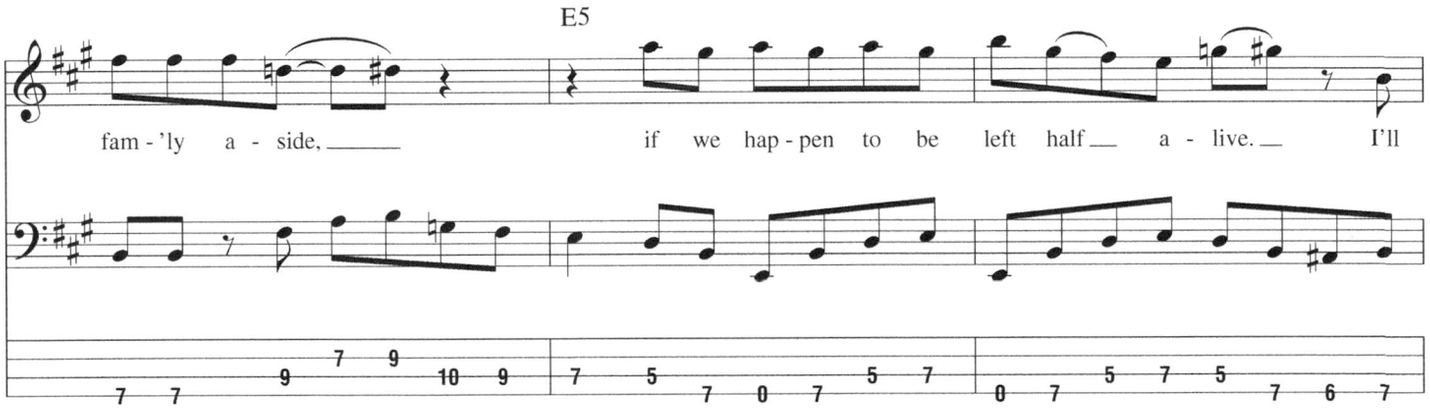
E5
fam - 'ly a - side, if we hap - pen to be left half a - live. I'll

A5
B5
get all my pa - pers and smile at the sky, oh, I know that the hyp - no - tized

Guitar Solo

A5

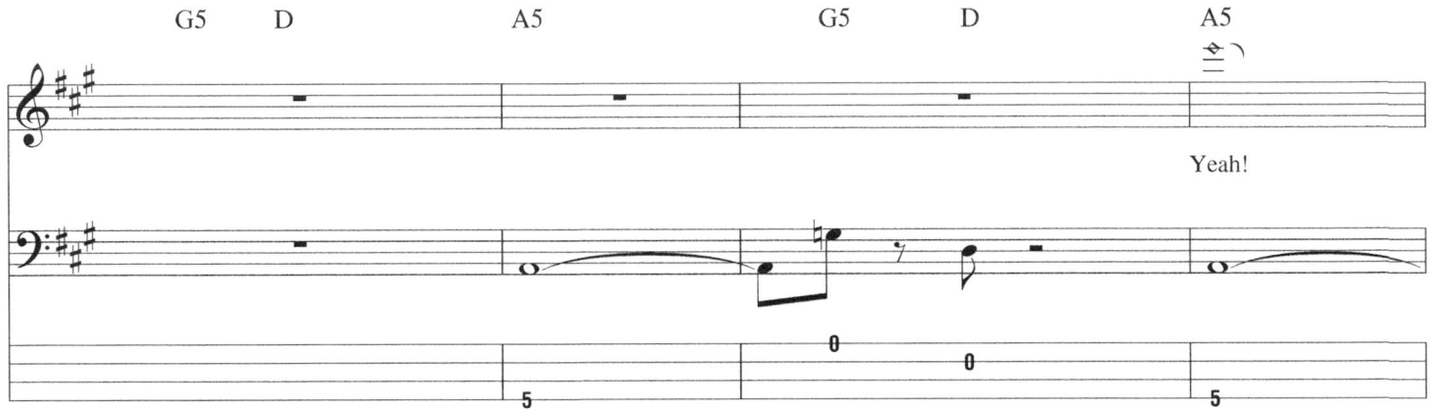
G5 D A5 G5 D A5
Yeah!

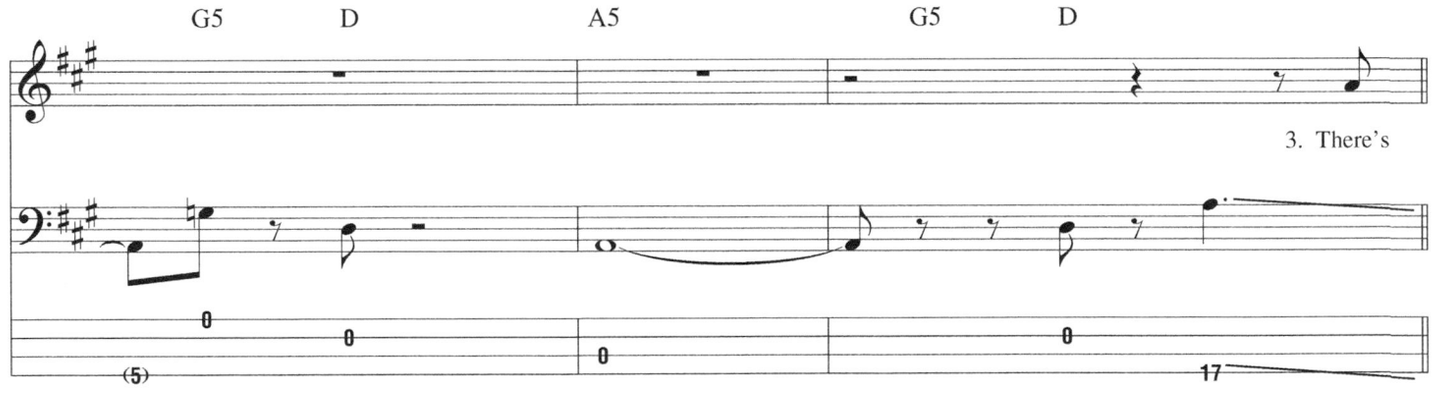
G5 D A5 G5 D
3. There's

Verse

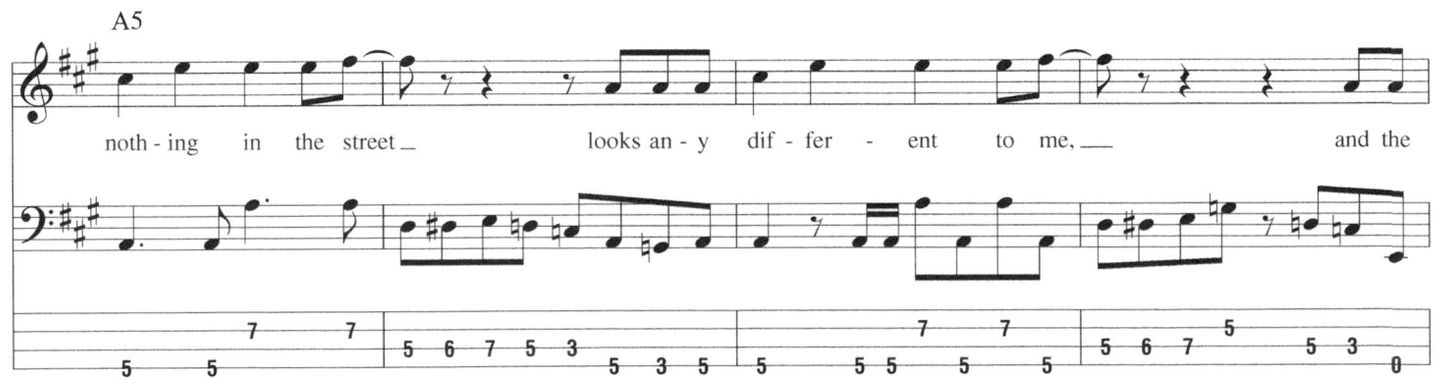
A5
noth - ing in the street looks an - y dif - fer - ent to me, and the

E
slo - gans are re - placed by the by.

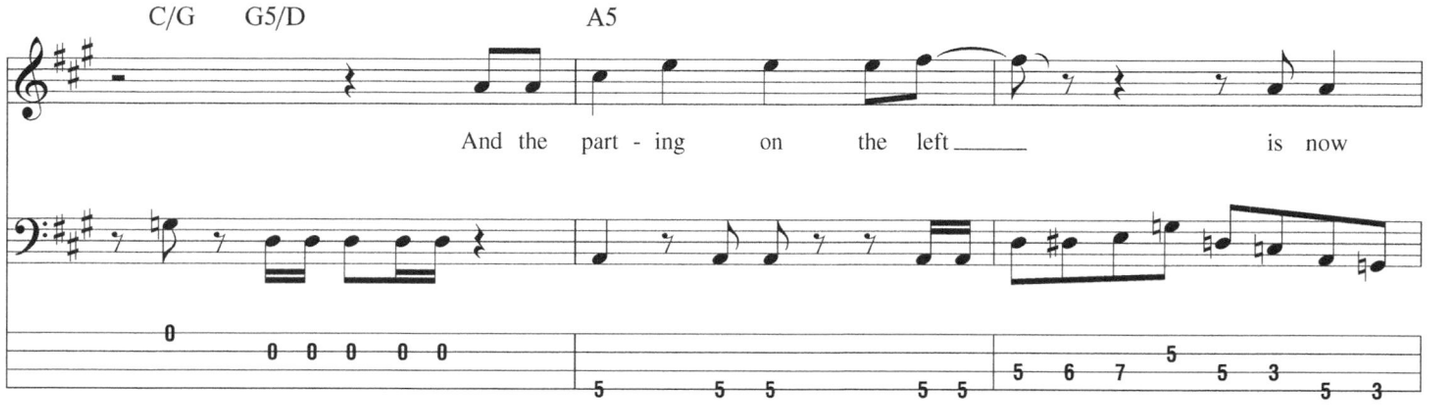
C/G G5/D
A5
And the part - ing on the left is now

part - ing on the right, and the beards have all grown long -

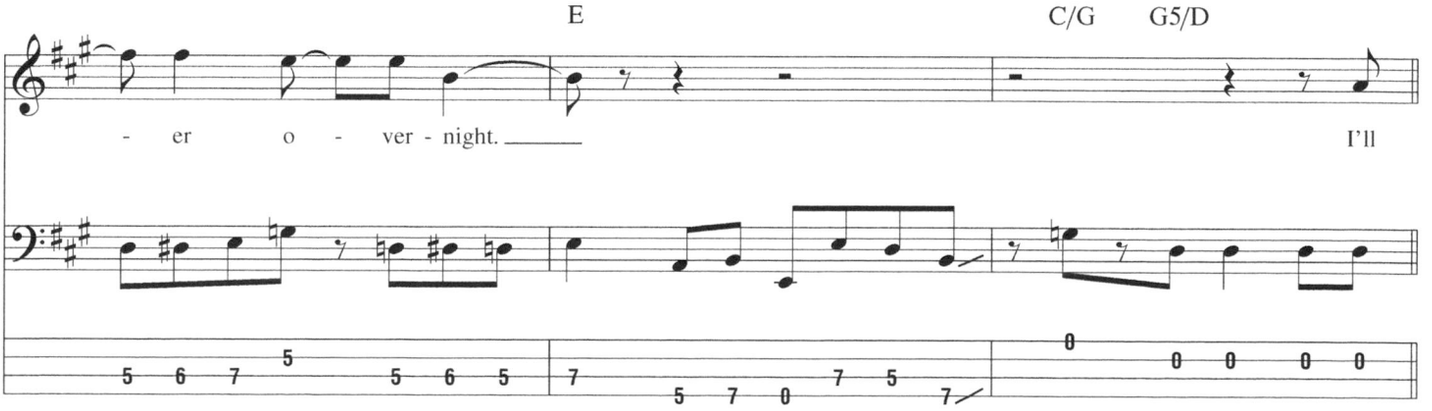
E
C/G G5/D
- er o - ver - night.
I'll

Chorus
D A5 D A5 D A5
tip my hat to the new con - sti - tu - tion, take a bow for the
D A5 D A5 D A5
new rev - o - lu - tion. Smile and grin at the change all a - round,
G E G
pick up my gui - tar and play, just like yes - ter - day,
E G D
then I'll get on my knees and pray

A5
we don't get fooled a - gain.
Don't get fooled a - gain.
No, no!
N.C.(A)

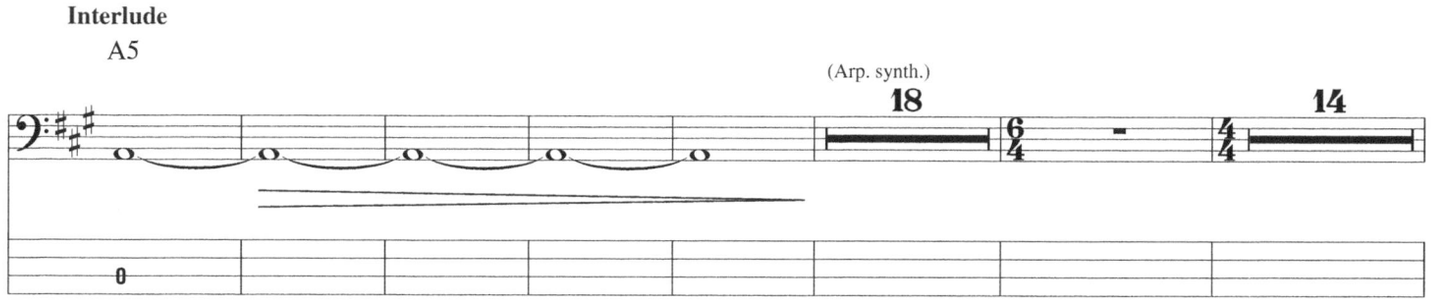
Interlude
A5
(Arp. synth.)
18
14

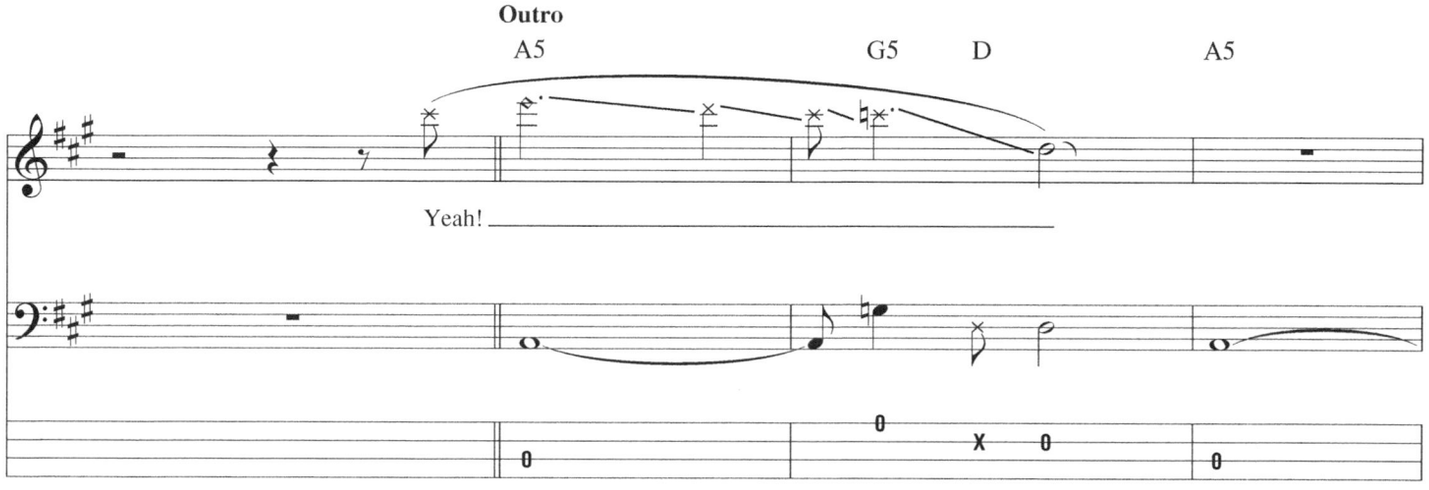
Outro
A5
G5
D
A5
Yeah!

G5
D
A5
G5
D
A5
Meet the new boss.
Same as the old boss.

G5
D
A5
G5
D

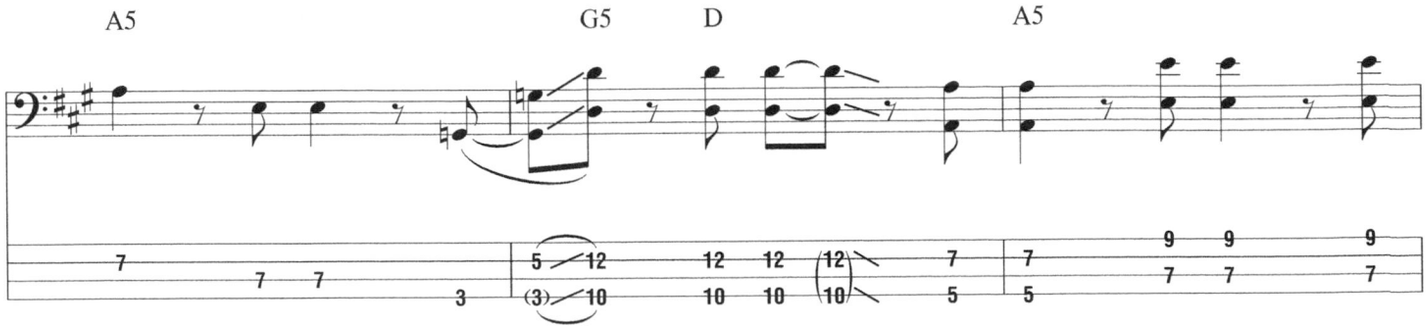

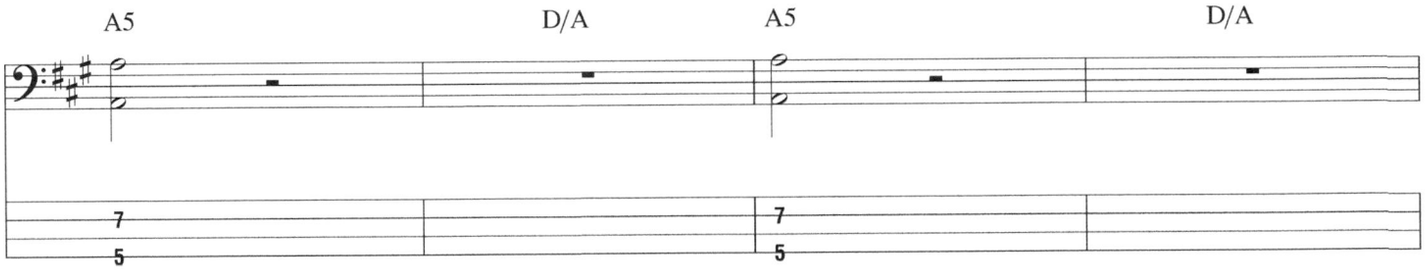

Free Time

Bass Notation Legend

Bass music can be notated two different ways: on a *musical staff*, and in *tablature*

THE MUSICAL STAFF shows pitches and rhythms and is divided by bar lines into measures. Pitches are named after the first seven letters of the alphabet.

TABLATURE graphically represents the bass fingerboard. Each horizontal line represents a string, and each number represents a fret.

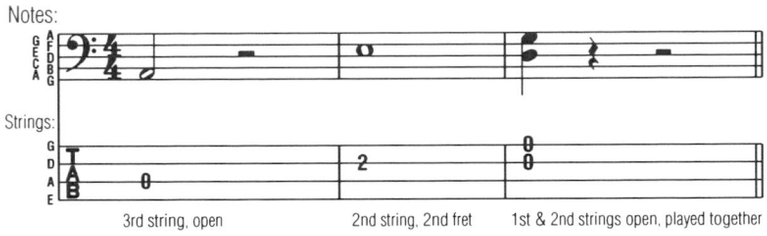

HAMMER-ON: Strike the first (lower) note with one finger, then sound the higher note (on the same string) with another finger by fretting it without picking.

PULL-OFF: Place both fingers on the notes to be sounded. Strike the first note and without picking, pull the finger off to sound the second (lower) note.

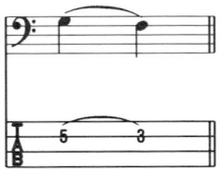

LEGATO SLIDE: Strike the first note and then slide the same fret-hand finger up or down to the second note. The second note is not struck.

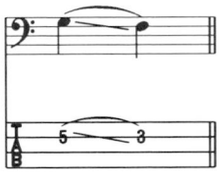

SHIFT SLIDE: Same as legato slide, except the second note is struck.

TRILL: Very rapidly alternate between the notes indicated by continuously hammering on and pulling off.

TREMOLO PICKING: The note is picked as rapidly and continuously as possible.

VIBRATO: The string is vibrated by rapidly bending and releasing the note with the fretting hand.

SHAKE: Using one finger, rapidly alternate between two notes on one string by sliding either a half-step above or below.

NATURAL HARMONIC: Strike the note while the fret hand lightly touches the string directly over the fret indicated.

MUFFLED STRINGS: A percussive sound is produced by laying the fret hand across the string(s) without depressing them and striking them with the pick hand.

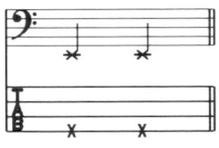

BEND: Strike the note and bend up the interval shown.

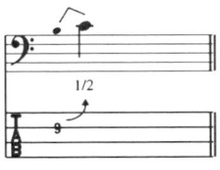

BEND AND RELEASE: Strike the note and bend up as indicated, then release back to the original note. Only the first note is struck.

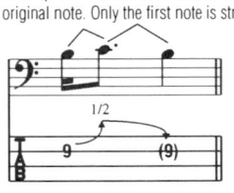

RIGHT-HAND TAP: Hammer ("tap") the fret indicated with the "pick-hand" index or middle finger and pull off to the note fretted by the fret hand.

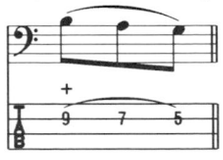

LEFT-HAND TAP: Hammer ("tap") the fret indicated with the "fret-hand" index or middle finger.

SLAP: Strike ("slap") string with right-hand thumb.

POP: Snap ("pop") string with right-hand index or middle finger.

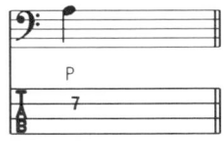

Additional Musical Definitions

(accent) • Accentuate note (play it louder)

(accent) • Accentuate note with great intensity

(staccato) • Play the note short

D.S. al Coda • Go back to the sign (𝄋), then play until the measure marked ***"To Coda"***, then skip to the section labelled ***"Coda."***

Fill • Label used to identify a brief pattern which is to be inserted into the arrangement.

• Repeat measures between signs.

• When a repeated section has different endings, play the first ending only the first time and the second ending only the second time.

HAL•LEONARD®

BASS PLAY-ALONG

The Bass Play-Along™ Series will help you play your favorite songs quickly and easily! Just follow the tab, listen to the audio to hear how the bass should sound, and then play-along using the separate backing tracks. The melody and lyrics are also included in the book in case you want to sing, or to simply help you follow along. The audio files are enhanced so you can adjust the recording to any tempo without changing pitch!

1. Rock
00699674 Book/Online Audio $16.99

2. R&B
00699675 Book/Online Audio $16.99

3. Songs for Beginners
00346426 Book/Online Audio $16.99

4. '90s Rock
00294992 Book/Online Audio $16.99

5. Funk
00699680 Book/Online Audio $16.99

6. Classic Rock
00699678 Book/Online Audio $17.99

8. Punk Rock
00699813 Book/CD Pack $12.95

9. Blues
00699817 Book/Online Audio $16.99

10. Jimi Hendrix – Smash Hits
00699815 Book/Online Audio $17.99

11. Country
00699818 Book/CD Pack $12.95

12. Punk Classics
00699814 Book/CD Pack $12.99

13. The Beatles
00275504 Book/Online Audio $17.99

14. Modern Rock
00699821 Book/CD Pack $14.99

15. Mainstream Rock
00699822 Book/CD Pack $14.99

16. '80s Metal
00699825 Book/CD Pack $16.99

17. Pop Metal
00699826 Book/CD Pack $14.99

18. Blues Rock
00699828 Book/CD Pack $19.99

19. Steely Dan
00700203 Book/Online Audio $17.99

20. The Police
00700270 Book/Online Audio $19.99

21. Metallica: 1983-1988
00234338 Book/Online Audio $19.99

22. Metallica: 1991-2016
00234339 Book/Online Audio $19.99

23. Pink Floyd – Dark Side of The Moon
00700847 Book/Online Audio $16.99

24. Weezer
00700960 Book/CD Pack $17.99

25. Nirvana
00701047 Book/Online Audio $17.99

26. Black Sabbath
00701180 Book/Online Audio $17.99

27. Kiss
00701181 Book/Online Audio $17.99

28. The Who
00701182 Book/Online Audio $19.99

29. Eric Clapton
00701183 Book/Online Audio $17.99

30. Early Rock
00701184 Book/CD Pack $15.99

31. The 1970s
00701185 Book/CD Pack $14.99

32. Cover Band Hits
00211598 Book/Online Audio $16.99

33. Christmas Hits
00701197 Book/CD Pack $12.99

34. Easy Songs
00701480 Book/Online Audio $17.99

35. Bob Marley
00701702 Book/Online Audio $17.99

36. Aerosmith
00701886 Book/CD Pack $14.99

37. Modern Worship
00701920 Book/Online Audio $19.99

38. Avenged Sevenfold
00702386 Book/CD Pack $16.99

39. Queen
00702387 Book/Online Audio $17.99

40. AC/DC
14041594 Book/Online Audio $17.99

41. U2
00702582 Book/Online Audio $19.99

42. Red Hot Chili Peppers
00702991 Book/Online Audio $19.99

43. Paul McCartney
00703079 Book/Online Audio $19.99

44. Megadeth
00703080 Book/CD Pack $16.99

45. Slipknot
00703201 Book/CD Pack $17.99

46. Best Bass Lines Ever
00103359 Book/Online Audio $19.99

47. Dream Theater
00111940 Book/Online Audio $24.99

48. James Brown
00117421 Book/CD Pack $16.99

49. Eagles
00119936 Book/Online Audio $17.99

50. Jaco Pastorius
00128407 Book/Online Audio $17.99

51. Stevie Ray Vaughan
00146154 Book/CD Pack $16.99

52. Cream
00146159 Book/Online Audio $19.99

56. Bob Seger
00275503 Book/Online Audio $16.99

57. Iron Maiden
00278398 Book/Online Audio $17.99

58. Southern Rock
00278436 Book/Online Audio $17.99

HAL•LEONARD®

Visit Hal Leonard Online at **www.halleonard.com**

Prices, contents, and availability subject to change without notice.

0222
334